india and south-e

the buddhist

india and south-east asia

the buddhist and hindu tradition

First published 1998 by
●●●ellipsis
55 Charlotte Road
London
EC2A 3QT
EMAIL ...@ellipsis.co.uk

ISBN 1 899858 42 3

© ellipsis london limited 1998

Publisher Tom Neville
Designed by Jonathan Moberly
Layout and image processing by Heike Löwenstein
Drawings by John Hewitt
Glossary by Andrew Wyllie
Index by Diana LeCore
Printed and bound in Hong Kong

British Library Cataloguing in Publication Data: a catalogue record for this publication is available from the British Library

contents

1 **Seal with bull device.**

Indus valley seals have been recovered from the stratum of a Sumerian site dated to the second half of the 3rd millennium BC, providing proof of contact between the two civilisations and the earliest guide to dating the cities of the Indus.

The history of India opens about the middle of the 3rd millennium BC, with one of the seminal civilisations of the world centred on several settlements in the valley of the Indus river and its tributaries. The remains of the two principal cities, Harappa and Mohenjo-daro, reveal a sense of planning based on a rectilinear grid and suggest a high standard of living for much of the population in substantial, well-drained courtyard houses. Bricks were standardised, and a wide range of objects recovered from the sites resemble those from Sumeria. Most characteristic are the finely worked steatite seals:[1] their inscriptions remain uninterpreted but their devices have been accepted as evidence for image worship involving the mother goddess, a horned deity, the phallus, the bull, trees and the genii of sacred spots. All these, and a great tank in the citadel at Mohenjo-daro,[2] foreshadow later Indian cults.

The Indus valley civilisation was overwhelmed about the middle of the 2nd millennium BC in one of the major upheavals of ancient Eurasia. Over succeeding centuries tribes of fair-skinned people originating from the steppes of central Asia entered India through the passes of the north-west. Related to the hordes who invaded the Aegean area at

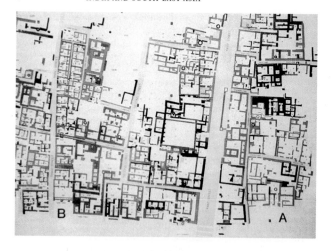

2 **Mohenjo-daro, Indus valley** plan of part of the site.
  Like Harappa and other cities of the Indus civilisation,
Mohenjo-daro was walled and dominated by a citadel
(to the west). Apart from the tank, the main buildings
excavated were a hall and a granary.

much the same time, they are known as Indo-Aryans.

The native people of India were settled in relatively advanced agrarian communities not unrelated to those of the Indus Valley civilisation. Their tradition, obsessed with fertility, was centred on the image-oriented worship of the mother goddess, but embraced the popular devotion to the water or tree spirit (naga and yaksha, female yakshini) of a sacred locality or object (chaitya). The invaders were nomadic herdsmen obsessed with the forces of the sky. Their tradition, enshrined in a series of compositions called Vedas, centred on propitiatory sacrifice at a fire altar in a sacred enclosure, principally of a potent mixture of fermented milk and vegetable juice called soma. With the slow infiltration of the subcontinent by the invaders, however, the pastoral and agrarian traditions gradually intermingled. The synthesis of the Vedic and native traditions, in particular the substitution of worship for sacrifice, is of prime importance in the evolution of India's religious architecture.

Vedic mythology and social organisation

The Vedas incorporated verses relating basic mythology. In the beginning Varuna, 'the unborn', floated on the cosmic ocean which held the germ of all existence, and the germ sent forth the tree of life through his navel. Varuna was identified as the Great Yaksha, and this was the crucial step in the synthesis of the Vedic and native traditions: yakshas controlled fertility and abundance for the natives, and they were to be accepted by Vedic writers as attendant on Varuna in the guardianship of the 'vital essence' of the waters. The yakshas guided the operation of this vital essence through its course from ocean to heaven and back to ocean in the infusions of sap, semen, and soma – the life of plants, animals and man, and the gods. Much of the embellishment of Indian buildings, religious and secular, incorporates fertility symbolism related to Varuna's tree and the generative power of water.[3-4]

In an alternative account, the Aryan storm god Indra, wielder of the thunderbolt,[5] vies with Varuna for the principal role in creation. The great warrior Indra slew the demon of evil and obstruction who held back the waters of life. The waters spilled forth, and Indra pegged earth to the floor of the ocean, propped up heaven with his staff, and released the sun to generate the cosmic cycle. In recognition of his

3 **Temple tank with lotuses.**

4 **Modhera, Surya Temple** sanctum portal.

The principal door frame (dvara) of the Indian temple was originally of several branches (shakha) tied together for strength. The main shakha usually represents its structure as the palace of the god (as here with the pilasters and lintel composed of multiple columned pavilions). Multiple accompanying shakhas rich with images of fecundity or generation establish the temple as a 'fording place' to new life (tirtha).

The lotus (padma) often stands as a symbol for Varuna's tree and for the unfolding universe, born of water-borne earth. The cycle of the waters laden with 'vital essence' is symbolised by the goose (hamsa) and the 'vital essence' itself by the crocodile (makara), the vehicle (vahana) of Varuna. Water is represented by the water pot (kumbha), or bowl (kalasha) which sometimes turns into the bulbous fruit of fecundity (amalaka). The bowl with lotus vines (padma-lata) trailing from its brim is the 'bowl of plenty' (purna-kalasha – as in the capitals of the pilasters here). The yaksha as armed defender (gandharva) represents guardianship of the 'vital essence'. Guidance of the 'vital essence' is represented by the yakshini as voluptuous female stimulator (apsara – as at the base and in the 'pavilions' of the pilasters here). Mounted on tree or crocodile, festooned with pearls – the richest fruit of the sea – she is the river goddess, consort of Varuna (as in the central niches at the base of the pilasters here). The stimulation of the male deity into activity by his consort is represented – often with sexual explicitness – by the 'productive couple' (mithuna), as in plinth and lintel here.

deeds he was made king of the gods – the 33 deities who took up residence on the primordial mountain, Meru, as creation diversified. Subsequent kingship stemmed from Indra's delegation of power to the first terrestrial ruler.

The early Vedic ruler, originally the patriarch of the extended family and leader of its warrior band, was seen to have the confidence of Indra so long as he fulfilled his obligations to protect the tribe from its enemies and foster its prosperity. Responsibility was to

5 **Indra and his standard** stupa railing detail from Bharhut (National Museum, Calcutta).

Indra's weapon is his thunderbolt (vajra) or pole (yashti), the standard of his imperium (dhvaja), the cosmic pillar (stambha) with which he established the law of the universe. It is the *axis mundi*, identified with the primordial mountain, Meru. Indra endowed the first earthly king, Vasu, with a pole as his standard. To ensure his potency in combat, each of Vasu's successors carried a pole surmounted by his own personal device into battle, and annually re-erected it in a hole or pot filled with water at a sacred spot in re-enactment of Indra's cosmic effort. It was similarly erected beside his burial mound in each case.

some extent shared by tribal councils, and the role of the priest was crucial, for victory and prosperity depended on his proper performance of sacrifice. With expanding nationhood and the weakening of familial ties, the pragmatic relationship between chief and people was supplemented, if never entirely supplanted, by the mystical one of god-given kingship – except in the foothills of the Himalayas where the tribal assemblies gained ascendancy in republics.

Vedic literature indicates that warriors, priests and commoners were recognised as distinct but not immutable classes – with the warriors dominant. Caste lines were drawn when the invaders, fearing the loss of Aryan identity, reduced the natives to slavery and proscribed interracial marriage. They gained religious sanction when the priests won supremacy over the warriors by means of the institution of hereditary monarchy and fostering the idea of the divine ordination of kingship: only the priests could invoke the 'motive power' of the divine through sacrifice.

Brahmanism

During the long period over which the Vedas were composed, the Aryans groped towards the comprehension of 'motive power', and identified it as Brahman – a concept not unlike the Numen of the Romans. Brahman may originally have been the magical power of the sacrificial formula – hence the priests, who laid exclusive claim to understanding the formula, were brahmins and their religion came to be called Brahmanism. If Brahman was the 'motive power' behind existence, the 'essence of existence' itself was identified as the Purusha. This had been undefined for aeons but was ultimately stirred by physical desire, and the Purusha's creative impulse was seen as self-sacrificial, with its division into male and female, good and evil, ultimately all the facets of existence. His male persona was Prajapati, the progenitor, and all the facets into which he was subdivided were personified as subsidiary deities.

Architectural theory

Prescribing the structure or embodiment of the Purusha (vastupurusha), Vedic literature provides the seminal corpus of Indian architectural theory, drawn upon by many compilers of professional treatises (shastras). An ordered complex, the vastupurusha is the macrocosm represented as the palace (prasada), city (ayodhya), or mountain (meru) of the gods. It is also the microcosm, man. The embodiment of the Purusha, comprehended through the dual study of man and the cosmos, may be represented in a diagram (mandala). Post-Vedic commentary elaborated mathematical and geometrical formulae for such a diagram to bind the Purusha to a specific place (vastupurushamandala)[6] for the purpose of worship – when worship succeeded sacrifice – and thus provided the

6 Vastupurushamandala.

The diagram is square because the earth, to which the Purusha is to be bound, is four-cornered in the supreme reality behind appearances where it is clasped by heaven, the points of contact manifest in the rising of the sun and moon, balanced by the poles. The figure defining man in perfect measure was also seen to be square (compare Vitruvius, Book IV.I).

The navel of Prajapati in the centre of the square is surrounded by the deified aspects of the sun and moon. Varuna and Indra reappear with Kubera (productivity) and Yama (death) as lokapalas (guardians of the four cardinal directions – west, east, south and north respectively).

In the planning and embellishment of the vastupurusha,

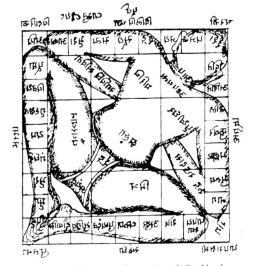

the movement of the sun and moon is symbolised by the
swastika. Their divergent courses are reconciled in the
embrace of Rahu (the eclipse), the recurrent cosmic sexual
act from which existence is reborn, symbolised by the
gaping leonine monster kirtimukha. The 'motive power'
behind existence is symbolised by the shardula (leogryph).

programme for any architectural exercise meant to accommodate that worship.

Late Vedism and the rise of unorthodoxy

Under the impact of changing circumstances in the first half of the last millennium BC, particularly the disturbing impact of settlement and native ways on their tribal traditions, the Indo-Aryans saw a stark contrast between the order embodied in the Purusha and their own rough passage through this world of flux. The conception of existence as cyclical – birth leading to death but death, itself illusory, leading to rebirth – promoted the belief that all forms of life are unified through the transmigration of souls repeatedly from one incarnation to another (samsara). From this followed the concept of moral order: that the deeds of each creature determine the level of its next existence (karma). Liberation (moksha) from the cycle of transmigration was to be obtained in the union of the individual soul with Brahman – but this was only available to the brahmin, the highest form of existence.

Enquiry into the nature of reality – especially the relationship between 'world soul' and the inner reality of the individual soul – is the unifying thread of the late-Vedic series of works known as Upanishads. Essentially unorthodox, their dominant trait is a profound humanity in their concern for the lot of the individual soul locked into the cycle of transmigration, and they culminate in a supreme statement of the salvation ideal, the sacred poem called the *Bhagavad-Gita*. Here the 'divine absolute' behind all natural phenomena, long deified, emerges as a personal deity whose grace is invoked to effect man's salvation through devotion. The consequences were profound.

The Mahavira and the Buddha

With their divinely ordained kings and powerful priests, the monarchies were naturally the centres of Vedic orthodoxy. The republics, on the other hand, tended to be favourable to the unorthodox. They provided fertile ground for the growth of religious reform movements inspired by the humanistic ideals of the *Bhagavad-Gita* in rejecting the exclusive pretensions of the priests of Brahmanism.

Among several unorthodox ways to liberation, the most important were offered by the Mahavira and the Buddha, princes of the 6th century BC. Each renounced his birthright for the privations of asceticism in the quest for salvation. The former proclaimed a doctrine concerned with the preservation of the intrinsically blissful soul through the renunciation of violent action – the way of the conqueror (jina) followed by the Jains ever since. The enlightenment of Siddhartha Gautama (the Buddha) followed the renunciation of soul itself.

Under the auspices of a renowned yaksha in a grove near Gaya,[7] the Buddha achieved enlightenment in the recognition of 'four noble truths': we are shackled to the cycle of existence in delusion and suffering; the cause is craving for worldly achievement in ignorance of the worthlessness of this world and in the mistaken belief in the existence of soul; the solution is the elimination of ignorance and the extinction of such craving; the way, effected through spiritual discipline (yoga), is the middle path between self-indulgence and self-mortification. The perfect follower of this path, the arhant, achieves blissful extinction in nirvana – the difficulty of defining which was to be the cause of much dissension.

With his first sermon on the 'four noble truths' (at Sarnath) the Buddha converted his audience and formed the nucleus of his order of monks (sangha). Shakyamuni (Sage of the Shakyas), for the rest of his

7 Bodh Gaya, Mahabodhi precinct.
A major end of Buddhist pilgrimage, a descendant of the pipal (bodhi) tree under which Prince Siddhartha Gautama (Buddha) achieved enlightenment, it is surrounded by many votive monuments. Beneath the tree, too, is the railing (vedika) protecting the promenade (chankyama) over which the Buddha deliberated with himself on the possibility of communicating his enlightenment to others.

life he travelled continuously throughout the Ganges basin, preaching his doctrine to all and expanding his following. On his death his body was cremated and the remains divided into ten parts, each of which was enshrined by its recipient in a tumulus (stupa). Venerated as sacred places (chaityas), these became the principal foci of Buddhist pilgrimage.

Having rejected extreme asceticism during his quest for enlightenment, the Buddha accepted for the sangha various endowments of land from lay followers anxious to acquire merit. Before long these supported monasteries (sangharama). The major monasteries were established at the scenes of the principal events in the Buddha's career, and the later embellishment of their shrines provides splendid images of the various building types, secular and monastic, in the Ganges vernacular.

Within the monasteries, in addition to canopies (chattris) protecting the sacred places, there were residential complexes of cells around a court or hall (viharas), often of several storeys (prasada or vimana),[8] and columned halls or pavilions for assembly (mandapas). Incorporating a chaitya with aisles and ambulatory for ritual circumambulation (pradakshina), the meeting hall became a shrine (chaitya-griha). The combination of pavilion or shrine and vihara, as in the 'Palace of the Gods' from Bharhut,[9] was an obvious development.

The Mauryas

The republics in which the Buddha and Mahavira had first found favour were sorely pressed by the time of their mature ministries. By the end of the 6th century BC, the King of Magadha, ruling from Pataliputra, had established the first empire in India by extending his sway over most of the Ganges basin. Nearly two centuries later Magadha had passed to Chandragupta Maurya. Confronting confusion in the west on the untimely death in 323 BC of Alexander the Great of Macedon – whose conquest of Achaemenid Persia had taken him all the way to India – Chandragupta came to terms with Alexander's successor Seleucus Nicator in Persia, and consolidated his control over the whole of north India. His grandson Ashoka (c. 270–232 BC) extended the empire to most of the subcontinent.

It is clear from the treatise on statecraft (*Arthashastra*) attributed to Chandragupta's chancellor Kautilya, that the Mauryas modelled themselves on the

8 **Ghantasala, stupa embellishment relief** multi-storey prasada called 'Palace of the Gods', 1st century AD?

A survey of numerous examples of such buildings found in the reliefs embellishing Buddhist monuments throughout India (by Coomaraswami in particular) suggests that in palaces, as presumably in monasteries, the upper levels

Achaemenids. Indeed, Persian craftsmen seem to have worked at the Mauryan court, providing the setting for the daily round of royal ceremonial. The provision of three distinct zones – for public audience, the king's private apartments and the enclosure of the royal women (harem) – had been the main concern of Persian royal architects, as it had with the Mesopotamians before them.

Chandragupta's palace at Pataliputra[10] doubtless combined the columned halls and multi-storey residential blocks of the timber vernacular, as in the relief of the 'Palace of the Gods', which was sustained by

contained the living quarters, often arranged in apartments. Usually walled only with lattices and lit by windows (gavaksha) with grilled shutters (jali), the storeys may be stepped back with full-length bay windows opening on to balustraded terraces often accommodating square or rectangular pavilions (kutagara). The ground floor, sometimes with recessed verandahs or porticos, was occupied by a reception hall or pavilion (mandapa) and service rooms. While prasada is a general term denoting multi-storey palatial buildings, vimana usually has a religious connotation.

9 **Bharhut, stupa embellishments** early 1st century BC, (ABOVE LEFT) mandapa-like gallery over Buddha's promenade at Gaya; (ABOVE RIGHT) end elevation of an aisled hall; (OPPOSITE) multi-storey vihara combined with chattri, inscribed 'Vijayanta Prasada' (identified with the 'Palace of the Gods' in Buddhist texts).

In the vernacular tradition, transition from post to beam was effected by brackets. Over the beams, a framework of bowed bamboo usually bore a thatched roof rising to a boss over square plans, and to a ridge pole over rectangles and projections. However, while bamboo and thatch are the materials most often mentioned in Vedic literature, wattle and daub seems also to have been common, and the reliefs suggest familiarity with brick and tile.

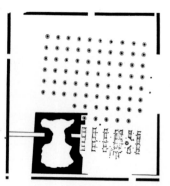

10 **Pataliputra, Mauryan palace** c. 300 BC, hall plan and capital.

Excavations at Pataliputra yielded monolithic column shafts, polished in the Persian manner, and a capital like those illustrated in the reliefs of Sanchi and Bharhut, but with volutes vertically disposed, as at the Persian dynastic cult centre of Persepolis, and adorned with decorative motifs of west-Asiatic origin long familiar in Persia. Also uncovered were the remains of massive timbers from a raft, upon which an apadana could have been sited.

11 Sarnath, Ashokan pillar

c. 270 BC, lion capital.

Originally surrounded by railings and circumambulatory path, the typical Mauryan pillar had an unfluted shaft rising from the ground to a tassel-like cap below an abacus embellished with goose or lotus and carrying an animal device symbolising royalty – a lion, a bull and an elephant have been found at various sites. The capital from Sarnath also has the equally royal horse, separated by chariot wheels, and four addorsed lions. It was once surmounted by the 'wheel of the law' which was set in motion by the Buddha's first sermon in the deer park at Sarnath. A similar capital was found by the Great Stupa at Sanchi.

secular rulers until comparatively recently. However, it was likened by contemporaries to Achaemenid Ecbatana, and the remains of its great hypostyle hall (apadana) – the earliest known stone structure in India – bear Persian masons' marks.

Moreover, the great Mauryas asserted their authority in edicts carved on rocks throughout their domains, following the example set by the Achaemenids at several sites in Persia. They also erected freestanding pillars (stambha) to serve a similar purpose. Though inspired in detail by the Persepolitan column (see volume 3, IMPERIAL FORM, page 18), their effectiveness depended on the religious significance of their age-old indigenous form: the pole of Indra, the *axis mundi*, the standard of kingship. Supporting both Buddhist and imperial devices – thus making it clear that the emperor saw Buddhism as a unifying force – Ashoka's pillars[11] were erected beside new stupas built throughout the empire to receive the remains of the Buddha disinterred from the original ten.

Sanchi: stupa and monastery

The veneration of images was foreign to early India, but Vedic ritual and the native yaksha cult of chaityas were readily adapted to the veneration of symbols, which took the form of walking around them clockwise (pradakshina) within a protective railing (vedika) modelled on the sacrificial enclosure. Predominant among these symbols was the stupa – a monument by its very nature.

The ubiquitous tumulus referred to in the Vedas, and often accompanied by the deceased's standard, seems to have been given its characteristic hemispherical form in India little earlier than the 6th century BC when the Buddha's remains were originally interred. The centuries between the death of the Buddha and the accession of Ashoka saw the refinement and elaboration of the primitive form, but it is impossible to say whether Ashoka was responsible for its final achievement of the precision, clarity and strength upon which monumentality depends. This is because, like their predecessors, most of his works have either been lost or enlarged and embellished under later rulers.

The Great Stupa at Sanchi is the prime surviving example of the type.[12] Its basic structure is Ashokan, but the railing defining the circumambulatory path (pradakshina patha), its four great gates (toranas)

12 OVERLEAF **Sanchi, Great Stupa.**

A Mauryan pillar capital found nearby indicates Ashokan foundation. The embellishment is generally thought to have begun c. 150 BC: sculptural style suggests that the southern ceremonial portal with Ashoka's pillar before it was the earliest and that the others followed over the next century. However, votive inscriptions suggest that work began with the northern gate early in the 1st century BC and that the others were completed before the end of the millennium.

In the first campaign of embellishment, the mound (anda) was enlarged to nearly twice its original size and given a plastered brick and stone envelope and a high drum (medhi) as its base. The top of the drum provided a railing-bordered terrace with a double ramp leading up to it on the south side. The new railing around the greatly expanded circumference at ground level, reproducing the timber original to a monumental scale, breaks forward at the four cardinal points to screen the entrances with their ceremonial portals surmounted by devices symbolic of Enlightenment. These portals still reflect the wooden prototype of the Vedic enclosure whose primitive portcullis was doubtless also surmounted by symbolic devices. Below the elephant capitals and accompanying bracket figures, the simple rectangular posts are incised, like the curved cross-beams, with magnificent reliefs depicting mainly mythical episodes from the career of the Buddha (Jatakas), which provide valuable information on early building.

The railing asserted that the stupa, no longer merely commemorative, had become a chaitya, an object symbolic of the Mahaparinirvana (the Buddha's attainment of nirvana). The second railing at the top of the mound specifically asserted the sacred significance of the cubicle (harmika) and the canopy (chattri) with its mast (yashti) crowning the stupa: the harmika probably initially contained the reliquary, while the chattri represents the honorific parasol due to the royal Prince Siddhartha Gautama and appropriated to the spiritual king, the Shakyamuni, which received its ultimate significance in superimposed tiers (chatavali) as the symbol of dharma, and thus became the 'chattri of chattris'. The mound and chattri were circular, the lower railing defined both circle and swastika, while the upper railing and harmika were square, prompting their later endowment with the symbolism of Vedic cosmology.

with their magnificent reliefs portraying incidents from the life of the Buddha (and conveying invaluable information on India's early building tradition), the reliquary cubicle at the top (harmika), and probably even the revetment of the mound itself (anda) were added over at least 100 years from the middle of the 2nd century BC – well after the disappearance of the Mauryas.

The sangha flourished with the patronage of rich merchants and the support of a large section of the working class, and monastic building proliferated even under the Brahmanical regime which supplanted the Mauryas. No early building now stands above foundation level at the principal Buddhist sites, except the stumps of the more important stupas, but Sanchi is particularly revealing in both the scale and scope of its remains.[13]

Rock excavation

Soon after their imperial patrons had inaugurated the Indian tradition of monumental masonry, but well before the acquisition of the skill to erect stone structures enclosing appreciable space, Buddhist monks sought permanence for their meeting halls and shrines

13 **Sanchi** plan of the monastic site.

(1) Stupa I – Mahastupa with Ashokan pillar to the right of the south portal; (2) Stupa III; (3) Temple 17; (4) Temple 40.

The foundations of Temple 40 include the earliest-known traces of a structural shrine (chaitya-griha), apsidal inside, rectangular outside. Temple 17 (see 30, page 76), considered to be the earliest-known masonry structure of its kind, dates from c. AD 450. The numerous smaller chaityas, halls, image chambers and viharas date from many periods, including the Mauryan.

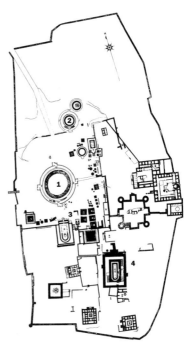

and viharas by carving them from the living rock. In
India, as in Dorian Greece, perishable forms sanctified
by association were translated literally into stone by
workers steeped in the craft conventions of carpentry.
But their overriding objective was the complete mas-
tery of the art of working in stone, not in structure, but
in sculpture.

Most impressive by far is the series of monasteries
hewn from the rock walls of the valleys in the western

14 **Ajanta** plan of monastic site (after Burgess, 1879, who
numbered the excavations 1 to 28 from east to west around
the bend in the Waghora river) and (OVERLEAF) view to the
north-east with shrines 9 and 10 right of centre.

Stone carving seems to have been mastered only after
at least a century of effort from the first attempts under
Ashoka in the Barabar hills. Dating, guided by the degree
of elaboration of form which may reflect practice in wood,
and less reliably by the degree of dependence on wood to
supplement the stone, is generally based on the somewhat
problematical analysis of the script and content of the many
votive inscriptions. Ajanta 10 has one of the earliest of
these, datable to the early years of the 1st century BC.

Work revived at the site in the second half of the 5th

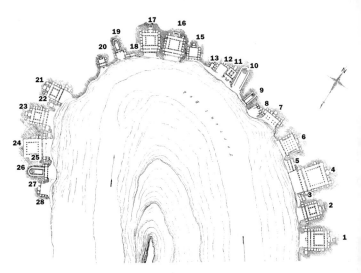

century AD under the later Vakatakas, though they were in
alliance with – indeed linked by marriage to – the Hindu
Guptas. In response to the transformation of Buddhism into
a theistic cult, two new shrines (19, 16) and associated
viharas (15–28) were excavated to the west of the original
ones (8–13) and another series added to the east (1–7).

15 **Ajanta, vihara 12** east range of cells.

Ghat,[14] through which the routes frequented by potential converts and patrons linked the centres of power in the north-west Deccan with ports on the Arabian Sea. There are a thousand significant excavations from the last century BC and the first two or three centuries AD at a score of sites. Ajanta, Bhaja, Bedsa, Karle and Nasik provide our examples. Most offer at least one shrine and several viharas, associated with each other as closely as the consistency of the rock permitted.

Working in detail from top to bottom, the carvers showed themselves adept at reproducing the intricate carpentry of extended halls and multi-storey residen-

16 OVERLEAF **Bhaja, chaitya-griha and vihara.**

Both datable to the early 1st century BC from similar inscriptions, the shrines of Bhaja and Ajanta 10 (see 14, pages 42–43) are comparable in their simple, slanting octagonal posts, without base or capital, and the irregular curve of their great arches. They originally had front screen walls entirely of wood, and support holes indicate that applied woodwork played an important part elsewhere in recreating the sort of detail to which stone did not immediately lend itself – such as galleries for musicians.

17 **Bedsa, chaitya-griha** section.

Votive records date back to the second half of the
1st century BC and the simple faceted posts separating
aisles from nave are not inconsistent with a relatively early
date. The Mauryan stambha order, used to screen the
verandah only, rises from a water pot to a petalled lotus (in
place of the tassel-like member), an abacus (encapsulating

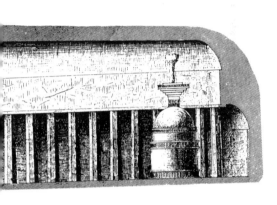

an amalaka) and addorsed animals (bull, horse and
elephant). The multi-storey vihara (vimana) carved on
the verandah walls in juxtaposition with the chaitya-griha
– as in the relief from Bharhut (see 9, page 29) – could hardly
be a more literal translation of the structural prototype
represented in the Bharhut 'Palace of the Gods'.

tial prototypes, with their railing-bordered terraces and balconies, lattice-screen walls, dormer and bay windows. The viharas[15] range from isolated cubicles to cells distributed regularly around a hall or court preceded by a portico. The typical chaitya-griha[16–17] is an elongated, unpartitioned hall with an apse containing the chaitya. Its façade, originally of wood, was later of stone, and aisles were separated from

18 **Karle, shrine** exterior and (FAR LEFT) interior.

The earliest votive records in the excavation at Karle seem to date from about the middle of the 1st century AD, after an apparent decline in activity at western Ghat sites for two or three generations. The last significant precedent was the magnificent shrine at Bedsa.

From a verandah, screened in stone, preceded by a monumental pillar after the Ashokan pattern, and later embellished in keeping with the development of Buddhism into a devotional theism, the nave and aisles were entered through three doors below an elegantly curved lunette. The Mauryan stambha order, following the Bedsa variant in the main, is used throughout (see 17, pages 48–49).

A similar order was widely used at most western Ghat sites in works generally later than the shrine at Karle.

nave with increasingly elaborate columns incorporating all the forms of the Mauryan pillar (see 11, page 31): the tassel-like element in the capital became an inverted lotus or water bowl, sometimes below a boxed amalaka, and a water pot protected the base of the shaft.[18–19]

19 Nasik, pillar from the Nahapana cave early 1st century AD.

An example of the Mauryan order, with water-pot capital and base.

Towards the end of the 3rd century BC, the Mauryas lost the north-western province of Gandhara to the kingdom of Bactria. Since the middle of the century Bactria's Greek rulers had been independent of the Seleucids, successors to Alexander the Great in the east, and they maintained close cultural relations with the west. By the end of the 2nd century BC Bactria had fallen to the Parthians, then masters of Hellenised Iran. The Parthians in turn were overrun by Scythian hordes from central Asia, but made a brief reappearance in Gandhara at the beginning of the 1st century AD. They were finally supplanted by another central-Asian horde, the Kushanas, who ultimately won the whole of north India from the Scythians, and controlled much of the great trade route which linked India through Persia to the Roman empire on the one hand, and to China on the other.

The impact on India of these eclectic invaders accelerated the 'great transformation' of Buddhism from a spiritual discipline to a devotional religion. In the face of the exclusive caste laws of Brahmanism, the invaders naturally espoused the heterodox cause. The prosperity fostered by their regimes favoured the merchants, who swelled the ranks of the Buddhist laity.

And the impulse was transmitted to the south where, following the Mauryas, the native Satavahanas had been enthusiastic patrons of Buddhism from the late-2nd century BC.

The Buddha made no supernatural claims, indeed he denied the idea of eternal soul, yet his followers could not believe him to be an ordinary man: within the space of two centuries the main stages of his career were seen as miraculous, and by the time of Ashoka devotion to the memory of a great teacher was well on the way to becoming worship of a transcendent being. The impulse came first from the lay followers rather than the sangha, though the way was prepared by dissension among the monks over the status of the laity.

The monks had given up all for the Buddha's way and their path was prescribed. The laity, still encumbered by the concerns of this world, were initially considered not to have fulfilled the condition for salvation, and in accordance with the prevailing orthodoxy seemed destined for transmigration. This was implicitly sustained by the Buddha in reputedly acknowledging that the laity would earn merit to improve their future lot by offering alms to the sangha and, adapting the age-old popular cult of yakshas at chaityas, through the veneration of symbols. However, seeing some ambiguity here in their teacher's attitude to the continuity of soul, the laity and their anti-clerical sympathisers within the sangha were readily convinced that the essentially compassionate Buddha had promised rebirth in heaven to those with faith in him.

The development of this popular theistic alternative to the yoga of the monk as a means to salvation – later called Mahayana (the Great Vehicle) and Hinayana (the Lesser Vehicle) respectively – depended upon the assertion that the compassionate spirit of Shakyamuni could not be unique. The populists postulated that in the infinite cyclical process of existence there had been, and would be, other aeons with other Buddhas. But, if Shakyamuni had not alone aspired to Buddhahood, then all might do so and, as compassion was at the heart of the Buddhist ideal, some aspirants would surely renounce their goal to take on the suffering of the devoted. These beings 'whose essence is enlightenment' are bodhisattvas. The most important were Avalokitesvara, the Lord of Infinite Compassion, Manjusri, the Helper to Enlightenment, Vajrapani, the Enemy of Evil, and Maitreya, the Buddha to Come.

With faith in the power of these ministering angels to break the cycle of transmigration on the devotee's behalf, not simply in recognition of merit won personally but through its transference, veneration turned to worship (puja). The venerable symbols of the Buddha were supplemented, then supplanted, by images of the Buddha and bodhisattvas formed after the example set by native yaksha cults and under the inspiration of Hellenistic anthropomorphic pantheism.[20]

The appearance of the image

The introduction of an image as the focus for popular devotion was the crucial step from the Hinayana to the Mahayana. The occasion was the patronage of the invaders, the Kushanas in particular, exercised through the sects within the sangha dedicated to the popularisation of the faith. Even before that, the advent of the Bactrians had brought from their Hel-

20 **Buddha, standing image from Gandhara**
2nd century AD.

The canon of idealisation and the toga-like cloak are both characteristic of the Indo-Hellenistic hybrid evolved in Gandhara.

lenistic background a tradition of monumental sculpture that represented god in terms of ideal man, just at the time when the Indians were beginning to make god out of man. Buddhist images seem first to have been applied to stupas, to represent the holy men whose remains were interred within – that is, the anthropomorphic idea of representation was superimposed over the abstract.

In the south, the Great Stupa at Amaravati was unexcelled in richness. Its mass has gone but much of its surviving revetment illustrates the phases of its evolution from the abstract to the representational.[21] The

21 RIGHT AND OVERLEAF **Amaravati, Great Stupa** elevations at three stages of development (last century of the Satavahanas from c. AD 130).

No Ashokan remains have been definitely identified in the south, even in the low mound which is all that remains of the Great Stupa at Amaravati, but a pillar fragment found nearby is sometimes linked with Ashoka's series. Vandalism and unscientific excavation have left little on site, but some 500 pieces of sculpted marble revetment, including differing representations of the stupa itself, give a clear idea of the monument's development.

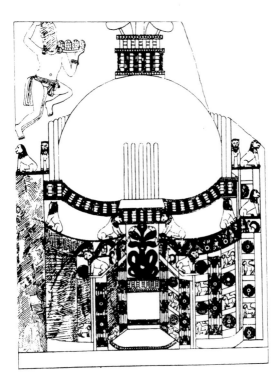

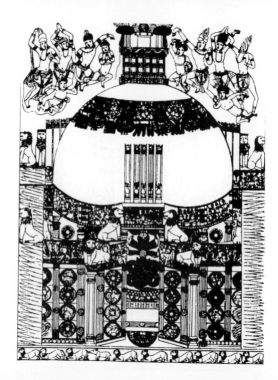

plastered mound, once unadorned, acquired relief panels in superimposed bands around its base and, finally, a rich garland towards its summit. It was set back from the edge of the relatively low circular drum, leaving room for a circumambulatory path – though there is no trace of access to the terrace. The drum, which had projections at the cardinal points bearing pillars (ayaka), was at first surmounted by a plain railing and adorned only with Hinayana symbols on the projecting wall below the pillars.

Ultimately, the reliefs representing the stupa were applied to all its walls below a magnificent frieze of legendary episodes from the life of the Buddha, relief panels were added to the railing, and the pillar projections received superb Mahayana images. On the outside of the circumambulatory passage about the base of the drum, another magnificent railing was finally decorated on both sides with floral or figural medallions, the greatest of the figural ones on the inside addressing the worshipper. The railing broke forward in two stages, before the projections at the cardinal points, to form lion-guarded entrances. Relief panels showing a simple stupa with a plain hemispherical mound on a circular drum seem contemporary with the representations of the Great Stupa in various phases of its elaboration and may represent, or even derive from, associated votive works.

In the north, such embellishment went along with elaboration of the stupa's form: drum was piled on drum to elevate the mound, plinth on plinth, and the chatravali was sent up to great heights with multiple discs. Other than the stumps of the main stupas and fragments of debased classical Orders converted to Buddhism,[22] little survives in the former domains of the Parthians and Kushanas, but the principle is well represented by votive stupas at the main sites in the Buddhist holy land (see 7, page 23) and rock-cut works in the western Ghats (see 14, pages 42–43).

Of new work undertaken for the service of the new faith, the most impressive was the product of a great Buddhist revival inspired by the triumph of the Mahayana in western India – new excavations at old sites, notably Ajanta[23–24] and Aurangabad, and comparable new effort at entirely new sites, notably Ellora and Bagh. The shrines retain their traditional plan but obsessive representation of obsolete structural detail gives way to anti-architectonic elaboration: beyond the multiplication of forms and the superimposition of

22 Sirkap (Taxila), Jamalgarhi Monastery debased Corinthian capital with Buddha inset centre (probably from the Kushana period).

23 Ajanta, shrine 19 probably c. AD 470, exterior.
The Mahayana shrines of Ajanta and Ellora (see 25, page 69) have fully developed entrance courts flanked by chapels. The single entrance of XIX is sheltered by an elegant portico of richly faceted columns crowned with amalaka and rising lotus mouldings (the bulbous and s-curved mouldings have western classical equivalents in the torus and cyma recta respectively). All retain a colonnade separating the circumambulatory passage from the hall and its sacred object.

images, essentially structural elements are transmo-
grified for symbolic effect. Arches take on the form of
Varunya's crocodile, for instance, and the tasselled
element of the Mauryan capital, already a lotus hang-
ing from an amalaka abacus at Bedsa, becomes a lotus
rising from an amalaka, or a water bowl with trailing
foliage (the 'bowl of plenty' – purna-kalasha).

From vihara to monastery

The introduction of Mahayana practice had its most
significant effect architecturally in the transformation
of the purely residential vihara of the Hinayana into a
place of worship. This was anticipated when cells were
endowed with stupas enshrining the remains of saintly

24 **Ajanta, shrine 19** interior.

  As on the exterior, the columns are removed from the
Hinayana prototypes by convoluted elaboration. The
shafts are many sided and bear floral or figural ornament
in varying degrees of relief below richly sculpted
representations of wooden brackets; but there is no lotus
rising from the amalaka capital except on the makara-
torana which shelters the Buddha on the front of the many-
tiered stupa.

former occupants, and a hybrid shrine type was evolved with an enlarged central cell dominating the hall. The main lines of development were concerned with the distinction of the shrine-chamber from a centralised hall surrounded by cells, often by the interpolation of a vestibule, providing for circumambulation. These were accompanied by iconographic developments which led to the eclipse of the stupa by the image of the Buddha standing protectively, seated cross-legged as the preacher of Sarnath, or enthroned as the universal ruler. The earliest surviving examples are rock-cut, as at Ajanta, Ellora[25] and Aurangabad,[26] but the development was anticipated in the monastic buildings of the north under the eclectic and heterodox rule of the invaders.

At the Gandharan capital, Sirkap (Taxila in modern Pakistan), the early viharas of the Dharmarajika Monastery were *ad hoc* groups of cells. Later, more regular walled quadrangles were surrounded by colonnades with one or two storeys of cells, some of which were converted into shrines.[27] The principal stupa was surrounded by small votive stupas and shrines, including the earliest-known image chamber (arca-griha).

25 **Ellora, vihara II** probably mid 5th century AD, interior.

A hall divisible into nine squares in plan, preceded by a vestibule, is characteristic of the Mahayana vihara shrines of Ellora and Ajanta. Columns are permutations of those encountered in the shrines – here with 'bowl of plenty' (purna-kalasha) capitals. Like the frames of the stupa images, shrine portals are occasionally anti-architectonic but the prasada motif is most common. The Buddha image here is of the universal ruler (Chakravartin).

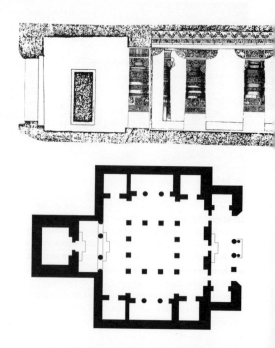

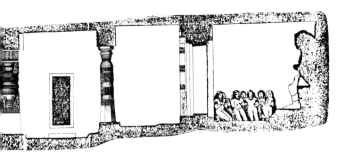

26 Aurangabad III probably late 5th century AD, section and plan.

Amalaka and purna-kalasha are fused on the columns defining a particularly sumptuous example of the nine-square hall, but on those before the door to the sanctuary the bulbous amalaka is combined with the opening padma. The Buddha image is again of the universal ruler and this was henceforth most common.

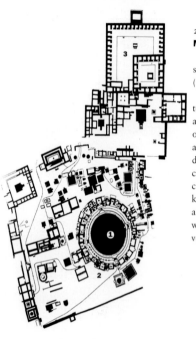

27 **Sirkap, Dharmarajika Monastery** plan.

(1) Mahastupa; (2) votive stupas and shrines; (3) viharas.

The Mahastupa seems to have been rebuilt with a considerable amount of earlier material after an earthquake which devastated the Parthian capital and its surroundings c. AD 30. The earliest-known building record of an image chamber, c. AD 78, was found in one of the votive shrines to its west.

28 **Sirkap** plan.

(1) Shrine; (2) palace.

After the earthquake of
c. AD 30, Sirkap was rebuilt
under the Parthians, but
the grid introduced by its
Graeco-Bactrian founders
persisted. With direct access
from the main street, the
great apsidal shrine catered
for the laity in accordance
with the liberal views of
the heterodox sects of the
sangha patronised by the
invaders. The remains of
twin stupas flanking the
entrance included fragments
of bodhisattva images
considered to be the earliest
found in India.

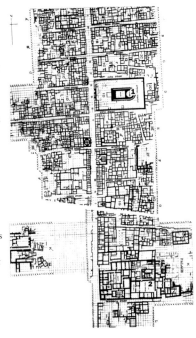

In Sirkap itself[28] excavators recognised the palace as an irregular variant on the court-and-iwan type of Parthian palace at Ashur, and they found fragments of Hellenistic Orders (see 22, page 64) debased in the manner characteristic of the Parthians in post-Seleucid Iran. A great apsidal shrine here marks an important development away from the orthodox tradition of the Buddhist sangha in the form of the erection of shrines for lay devotees, independent of a monastic establishment. At near-by Jandial, moreover, are the remains of the earliest freestanding temple so far discovered in India: the 'Fire Temple'.[29] Its similarity to the typical Roman form is striking.

Early temples

The earliest intact temple in India, built about AD 450 at Sanchi in magnificently dressed masonry, is hardly different in form to the primitive image chamber of Sirkap: a square cella for the deity preceded by a little portico to shelter the worshipper.[30]

From this point on, the development of Indian temple architecture is in principle very simple. With the advent of the anthropomorphic deity came the need to provide him with a house – a vastu, represented by a

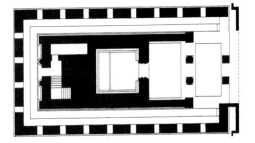

29 **Jandial, so-called Fire Temple** late 1st century BC?, plan.

Built of coursed rubble in a manner familiar from the Shakha period, well before the earthquake of c. AD 30, this important work has been identified as Zoroastrian. The capitals were Ionic rather than the debased Corinthian more common in Gandhara (see 22, page 64).

30 **Sanchi, Temple 17** c. AD 450, view from north-west.

The flat-roofed cella (mulaprasada) and porch (praggriva) are bound by a continuous architrave and based on a simple stepped stylobate. The columns still clearly conform to the Mauryan type, suggesting that this is the oldest of a series of similar works, including the temple at Tigawa and several at Udayagiri (near Sanchi), in which the tassel-like member of the capital has become a 'bowl of plenty'.

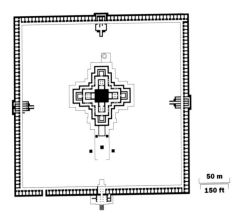

31 **Paharpur** late 8th century, plan.

Multiplication of the elements of the standard formula –
as represented by the Mahabodhi Temple at Bodh Gaya –
produces a cruciform plan with porches and halls on all four
sides of the square cella. On three terraces, the form of the
superstructure is not clear.

32 **Bodh Gaya, Mahabodhi Temple.**

Probably founded in the 6th century but subject to many restorations, several at the instigation of the Burmese including the last in the late 19th century, the temple still resembles the building described by the Chinese Buddhist pilgrim Hiuen Tsang in the 7th century: 'to the east of the bodhi tree was a temple above 49 metres (160 feet) high and with a front breadth at the base of more than 20 paces. This temple was made of bricks and coated with lime; it had tiers of niches with gold images; its four walls were adorned with exquisite carvings of pearl strings and genii; on the roof was a gilt copper amalaka; connected with the east side of the temple were three lofty halls one behind another.'

The principal image chamber, preceded by a prominent porch, is uncharacteristically built on arches. The zone of circumambulation around the cella is reflected in the open terrace above a second cella. The multi-storey prasada clearly provided the model for the superstructure, each storey dominated by a dormer which penetrates the zone of the one above. At the corners of the terrace small replicas of the main shikhara were constructed during the most recent restoration, apparently on analogy with the remains of the temple at Nalanda of which Hiuen Tsang wrote: 'in size and ornamentation and in its image of the Buddha this temple palace. Indeed the temple in India is the palace of the god and is composed of the two major elements found in the palace of the king: the residential tower-block (prasada) and the audience hall. Multiplication was the key to development: of the number of halls – as at Paharpur[31] – or the number of storeys of the prasada – as at Bodh Gaya.[32] And, like many others, the Indians modelled their approach to worshipping the god on the way they would honour the king.

resembles the one at Bodh Gaya'. It is not clear whether the Burmese influenced or were influenced by the stupa which crowns the edifice with its chattravali in the form of a ringed cone: it predates the latest restoration but matches the Burmese type.

The success of Buddhism and the gradual emergence of the Mahayana prompted a reform movement from within Brahmanism itself which led to the great religion later to be called Hinduism. Rejecting the claims of the Vedic priest and his abstruse mystical sacrifice, but inspired by the native holy itinerant, the most progressive minds sought liberation through meditation aided by severe, still mystical, discipline and the life of the ascetic. But liberation was remote from the popular level, and the masses, committed to the cycle of transmigration and the wages of former deeds, sought more immediate comfort from the hope offered in later Upanishadic thought, by the *Bhagavad-Gita* in particular, that divine grace could be invoked through devotion to a personal god. In a process parallel to the demotion of yoga and the eclipse of the monk in Buddhism, well before the end of the 1st millennium BC sacrifice had receded in importance before the growing belief in the efficacy of worship.

In the synthesis of late Vedism and native popularism, many lesser Vedic gods were endowed with the properties of native fertility deities. Shiva – an associate of the old god of death – and Vishnu – an attendant on the sun god – emerged predominant. Together with the personification of the Purusha (the 'essence of existence'), Prajapati (who embraced Brahman – the 'motive power' behind existence – as Brahma), they formed a trinity governing the cycle of creation, preservation and destruction.

Responding to the same popular needs as the Mahayana, the most important strand in the development of Hinduism in the last half of the 1st millennium AD was the descent of the deity from transcendence to immanence. This was effected by the god's consort and activator (shakti), who descends directly from the age-old indigenous mother goddess, the feminine power of fertility. From the premise that cosmic force is generated by the interaction between male and female, heterodox shakti sects developed the radical tantric way to salvation in the ritual breaching of sexual taboos – and made a distinct impression on temples.

Sectarian devotion crystallised around Shiva and Vishnu – naturally, as preservation and destruction are the immediate concerns of the living. As represented at Elephanta,[33] Shiva is a complex of the fearsome and the benign. The great lord (Maheshvara), whose procreative and potentially destructive energy motivates the cosmos, he is the omnipotent, all-comprehending

Trimurti, worshipped through the phallus (linga) and carried by the bull (Nandi) inherited from his pre-Vedic ancestors. He is most persuasively Nataraja, 'lord of the dance', whose 108 permutations of rhythm encompass all the phases of the cosmic cycle. But in his mountain fastness of Kailasa he is the comprehender of order as the equipoise of the forces of creation and destruction, Dakshinamurti, the universal teacher and patron of ascetics, the fountain of art.

At Deogarh,[34] the progress of Vishnu and his consorts is shown in some detail. Awakening from sleep on the coils of Shesha, the thousand-headed snake, in the primordial ocean when Brahma – the instrument of creation – emerged in a lotus from his navel, Vishnu became Narayana, the promoter of creation: the old role of Varuna. The blast from his conch stimulated life from the primordial sea, the trajectory of his discus at once generated time and menaced destruction. Carried on the man/eagle Garuda to his residence on his holy mountain, Vaikuntha, he observes the world, descending to save it in the various heroic and

33 OVERLEAF **Elephanta, Great Shiva Temple** late 6th century, Shiva Maheshvara (also called the Trimurti).

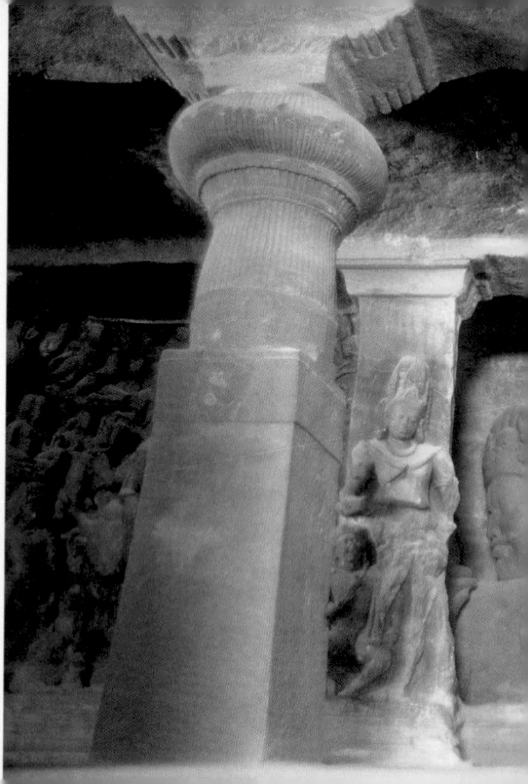

34 **Deogarh, Dashavatara Temple** Vishnu Narayana.

benevolent incarnations (avatars) through which he is worshipped.

Sri Lakshmi, the consort of Vishnu and goddess of good fortune – seen at Deogarh with her sister river goddesses in attendance on Narayana – was among the treasures redeemed from the ocean by the god in his avatar of the tortoise Kurma. Her origin as an apsara (female stimulator) descended from the mother goddess is clear: she was, indeed, the consort of Varuna as lord of the waters.

The consort of Shiva, Mahadeva (the great goddess) – shown at Deogarh with Shiva on the bull Nandi in attendance on Narayana – is naturally ambivalent in character. As Mata and Annapurna she is the great mother and abundance. In the most benign of her aspects she is Gauri the Pure, Sati the Virtuous, Parvati the Daughter of the Mountain, and may be identified with Varuna's river-goddess consort as Ganga flowing from the mountains around Kailasa, the very source of shakti. As Minakshi she is the daughter of Kubera, defender of the faith, who himself entered Shiva's service on Kailasa. But she is also the savage Durga and the bloodthirsty Kali.

The product of a syncretic process and embracing a

wide range of roles and powers, the multiple identities of the Hindu deity in a multiplicity of forms distance the icon – never a mere image but a potential seat of grace – from the realities of this inadequate world of appearances. Thus hybrids endow the figure with the attributes of relevant animals, and multiple heads and arms express their super-human importance. Meanwhile, the details of human physiognomy cede to an idealisation, governed by Brahmanical prescription, ultimately promoting a formula for supreme beauty and arousing sexuality. Transitory human emotion and the accident of personality are equally irrelevant. Transcendent facial expressions, rather, invoke character – the principal aspect of the deity as benign and compassionate or terrible and compelling, for instance – and these are reinforced through hand gestures reflecting the attitudes that underlay the earliest representation of transcendent being for the Buddhists.

Beyond this, identity is established in the attributes of a particular manifestation of the deity, from the vehicle (vahana) accompanying them, through their weapons, to the whole corpus of shakti symbolism deriving from the 'water cosmology' and the image of Shiva's procreativity, the phallic linga. The deity's power is most graphically portrayed in episodes from the rich mythology inherited by Hinduism from the Vedic past, chosen as significant of divine intervention.

Together with their shaktis, both Shiva and Vishnu ultimately gained vast followings to the almost total exclusion of the daunting Brahma, the originator. Under the broad cloak of Hinduism, however, the sects were largely tolerant of each other, none denying that the object of their devotion was an aspect of a single divinity, as both preservation and destruction comprehended creation and implied one another. Thus room was found for all the Vedic deities as well as a wide variety of popular cults – and tantrism. Buddha was recognised as the ninth avatar of Vishnu, moreover, and the Mahayana was gradually absorbed by Hinduism until the final blow was dealt to the Indian sangha in the 13th century by the Muslim invaders who set themselves to extirpate monasticism and the outrageous practices which they believed it fostered.

The decline of Buddhism

The decline of the Buddhists in India began when the Kushanas ceded most of their territory in northern India to local powers. The lower Ganges basin went to the Gupta, a Maghdan family with Mauryan pretensions who re-established Pataliputra as an imperial capital early in the 4th century AD. They ousted the last foreign rulers from western India and built up an extensive system of contractual relationships. Knowing a longer period of peace and consequent prosperity than any other rulers since Ashoka, they presided over the maturity of one of the greatest phases in Indian cultural history. The dynasty was Hindu and under its patronage – and that of its Vakataka allies in the northern Deccan – the basic forms of the Hindu temple were stated in the most refined terms.

Dynastic rivalries

Undermined by protracted fighting with new tribal invaders led by the Huns, by the end of the 5th century AD the Gupta had lost control over their clients. Despite brave attempts, no lasting empire was to emerge in the north for several centuries, though in the Deccan by the end of the 6th century the Chalukyas had built a considerable one on the ruin of the Vakatakas. Meanwhile, the south was falling to the Pallavas of Kanchipuram who presented themselves as rivals to the Chalukyas. Their protracted conflict was indecisive as power and fortune were equally matched, but it fostered interaction between Aryan and non-Aryan cultures.

Finally exhausted by the forces of Islam pressing in with Arab traders from the west, the Chalukyas succumbed to the Rashtrakutas, their former vassals, in the middle of the 8th century. The Pallavas lasted more than a century longer. Their conquerors, the Cholas of Tanjavur, initially fostered a Chalukyan revival to the cost of the Rashtrakutas. The zenith of Chola power was reached in the first half of the 11th century. Their ambitions conflicted with those of the Later Chalukyas, and though the latter succumbed towards the end of the 12th century, the Cholas were unable to resist the rise of new dynasties in the Deccan – particularly the Yadavas of Devagiri and the Hoysalas of Dorasamudra. From the mid-13th century the Pandyas of Madurai were supreme in the south until absorbed by Vijayanagar into the last great Hindu empire. In its turn Vijayanagar was to be extinguished by the Muslims towards the end of the 16th century and divided between its former viceroys (nayakas).

In the north, meanwhile, the Pratiharas had emerged predominant from among the clans of the

Gujara tribe – generally called Rajput – who had entered northern India in the wake of the Huns. They built their power on successful resistance to the Arabs but weakened it in rivalry with their southern and eastern neighbours, particularly the Buddhist Palas of Bengal. The latter succumbed to conflict with the great Cholas in the 11th century and were replaced by a succession of Hindu dynasties in the north-east of the subcontinent, most notably the Somavamshis. About the same time in the north-west, the Pratihara inheritance was divided between other Gujara clans: from our point of view the most important were the Solankis of Gujarat, the Paramaras of Malwa, the Chandellas of Bundelkhand and the Chahamanas who asserted their suzerainty over lesser Rajputs in Rajasthan – but the ultimate beneficiary was Islam.

The Hindu deity is worshipped in the form of an image or symbol sanctified to fit it for the god's residence. Like a supreme personage, the deity incumbent in the image is awakened from the sleep of non-manifestation, greeted with flowers, bathed, anointed, dressed, fed, honoured in accordance with the tradition of circumambulation, entertained with dancing, confined with his wife, and paraded through the town in a glorious car (ratha) on festival holidays. As worship is primarily the sacrifice of service and sustenance by the individual worshipper or, more regularly, by the priest whose caste fits him to represent the faithful – as in the earliest native cults – it requires the provision of little more than the basic elements of the image chambers we have already encountered at Sanchi (see 30, page 76). Hand in hand with the development of Hinduism, indeed, went the development of the temple from Buddhist precedents.

Among the rare works contemporary with Temple 17 at Sanchi (c. AD 450), the Hindus are generally credited with several part-built, part-excavated shrines at Udayagiri near Sanchi, which also consist of cella and porch. By far the most significant surviving early structural temple of the type is the Dashavatara at

3 5 PREVIOUS PAGES **Deogarh, Dashavarata Temple** from the south-west.

Usually assigned to the 6th century on stylistic grounds, the temple bears an inscription attributable to Govinda Gupta, Viceroy of Malwa, for his brother the emperor Kumara Gupta (415–54) who took the era to its apogee.

The broad podium, with steps at the cardinal points, carries a five-shrine (panchayatana) complex. Single projections accommodating the magnificent five-jamb portal and the blind doors with their splendid reliefs (including the Narayana to the south) are embellished with an Order in which the 'bowl of plenty' replaces the Mauryan capital throughout. The podium and the socle of the cella have a simple range of mouldings that persisted throughout the history of the Hindu temple, despite later augmentation and elaboration with lotiform motifs in particular. The main floor slab was given a rounded top, presumably to protect it (the form was called khura after its supposed resemblance to a hoof); above that was a torus (kumbha) and a cornice moulding echoing the form of the eaves (kapota), which – to those attuned to arcane symbolism – recalled respectively the water pot and tortoise. A superstructure of graded tiers projects in response to the frontispieces: it may have been the first of its kind.

Deogarh[35] where we encountered Vishnu Narayana (see 34, page 86). Most spectacularly, they followed the example of Mahayana excavators at several sites in the north-west Deccan and the south: their main theme was the vihara temple, and the supreme variant was the Great Shiva Temple at Elephanta[36] where we encountered the Trimurti (see 33, pages 84–85).

The vihara and even the apsidal shrine were occasionally recalled in monumental masonry – most notably at Aihole[37] – but the typical Hindu temple is a succession of rectangular, indeed square, volumes. In general, a cella enshrining the image, often with ambulatory, vestibule (antarala) and porch to shelter the worshipper, was set in a precinct with at least one pavilion for dancing and banqueting.[38]

The role and form of the temple

The temple increased in complexity with the elaboration of the iconographical programme in response to the development of the religion itself. However, the complex goes far beyond provision for worship: as the nucleus of the community, as hospice and hospital, sanctuary and school, its expansion over the centuries provided the facilities needed to feed and shelter

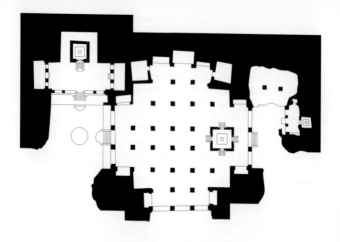

36 Elephanta, Great Shiva Temple late 6th century, plan.

The Hindus and Jains followed the Mahayana example in excavated temples at several sites in the north-west Deccan, notably Badami, Ellora and Elephanta. Their earliest efforts repeated the latest Buddhist forms, but the centralised pattern of cells priests, poor and pupils as well as the extensive bureaucracy that handled its endowments, managed its estates, administered its charities and employed its servants. Moreover, given no clear distinction between Hindu religious and secular life, it is the centre of intellectual and artistic effort, promoting the development of painting, sculpture, architecture and the performing arts as well as philosophy and theology.

Above all, as the house of god, the theatre for the sacrifice of service and sustenance, the temple is a place

around a hall was suppressed as they became surer in meeting their own non-monastic needs and the problem of circumambulation about one dominant shrine opposite the entrance was resolved.

In their culminating achievement at Elephanta two axes were reconciled: the main axis runs through a rectangular hall from the Nandi statue and the entrance (west) to a four-faced shrine-chamber (east); the secondary north–south axis, depending on the columns dividing the portico and vestibule, leads from a southern entrance to the Trimurti. Elaboration of both the 'bowl of plenty' and padma-kumbha type of column appealed to the Hindus no less than to the Buddhists.

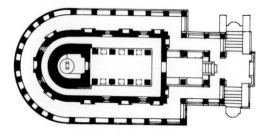

37 Aihole, 'Durga Temple' probably originally dedicated
to the sun god Surya (late 6th or early 7th century?), plan
and view from the south-west.

   In an elegant variation on the Buddhist chaitya-griha
(not without precedent in Chalukyan domains), an apsidal
cella encloses both hall and sanctum with ambulatory and
is itself embraced by a colonnaded gallery which forms a
second ambulatory.

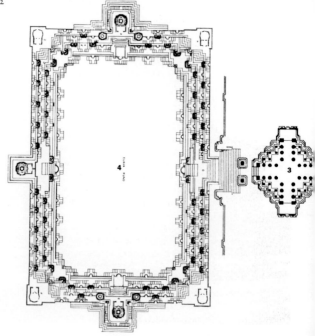

38 Modhera, Surya Temple datable from an inscription of 1026, plan.

(1) Cella with ambulatory around sanctum; (2) closed hall with porch; (3) open hall preceded by ceremonial gate; (4) tank.

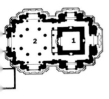

Heirs to much of the original Pratihara domain, the Solanki kings ruled most of north-west India from the early 11th century until the triumph of Islam there two centuries later. They were prolific builders on the proceeds of trade through the rich ports of Kathiawar and Gujarat. Exposed to the full force of Muslim iconoclasm, their achievement at its peak is represented only by fragments, of which the Surya Temple at Modhera, by no means the most extensive, is the most substantial. Nowhere is the decorative elaboration of all the elements – base, walls, columns, portals – more fecund.

of epiphany where the operation of god's grace, his descent from transcendence, is effected through the shakti. Thus its sanctum in the cella is called womb chamber (garbha-griha) because the gestation of grace takes place there through the intercourse of the god and his shakti. Its door is an elaborate proscenium for the deity's display: reflecting the palace imagery of the structure itself, it perpetuates the identity of god in epiphany and king in audience.

The temple is also a place of pilgrimage. Ideally pilgrimage is to the holy waters at a spiritual fording place (tirtha) providing purifying and regenerative passage as initiation to salvation. Thus the temple is a tirtha and its natural site is by the sacred waters of a river – and often is, in practice. If, exceptionally, water is not present on a site whose auspiciousness is indicated by signs of divine favour, it is ritually introduced to the sanctum by means of immuring a pot or bowl (kumbha or kalasha) during the consecration rites and tanks are constructed to collect rain water for the obligatory ritual ablution. Passage through the waters is symbolised in a succession of portals rich with the images of fertility (see 4, page 12) – notably the river goddesses Ganga and Yamuna, and lush lotus vines entwining couples engaged in sexual intercourse (mithunas).

The spiritual momentum generated culminates for the priest in communion with the deity in the womb chamber itself. However, divine grace emanates from the womb chamber to endow the devotee at the portal, and the principal aspects of the deity (parshva devatas) – the three persons of the trinity, avatars of Vishnu, faculties of Shiva, or the shakti – are manifest in blind doors (ghanadvaras) at the cardinal projections (see 34, page 86). Stepping forth from numerous smaller aedicules are subsidiary members of the pantheon (avarana devatas) – above all the guardians of space (ashtadikpalas) and regulators of time, controllers of the destinies of men. These Shaktis permeate the temple by means of symbols of the water-pot, lotus and tortoise, representing heaven and earth born of water. All three are reflected in the torus (kalasha or kumbha), cyma recta (padma) and pointed astragal (karnaka) mouldings which separate rectangular floor and base slabs. The same mouldings reappear in capitals, especially of pilasters, the ribbed amalaka having become the smooth kumbha below a comparably simplified lotus.

The residence of the Purusha

At its climax, the momentum developed along the ground plane shoots upwards to send a kalasha-crowned superstructure rearing to heaven. After the superimposition of receding slabs over the primitive rectangular cella, the cosmic form of the Purusha's residence was first seen as the multi-storeyed prasada or vimana of palace or monastery, as at Bodh Gaya (see 32, page 78), then as the holy mountain – Meru or Vishnu's Vaikunta or Shiva's Kailasa.

Representation, rather than structural innovation, was always the main concern of Hindu builders, above all the constitution of the residence of the Purusha in accordance with the Vedic ideal of reproducing the form of the cosmos (see 6, page 19). Thus the vastupurushamandala was central to the Hindu science of architecture (vastushastra), and guaranteed that, despite regional differences in materials and methods, there was a strong measure of consistency in the conception of the temple throughout the subcontinent.

Southern temples

Reproducing carpentry in monumental masonry, the image of the Purusha's residence as the multi-storeyed

39 OVERLEAF **Mahaballipuram, rathas** mid 7th century, (left to right) Draupadi, Arjuna, Bhima and Dharmaraja.

The single-storey Draupadi, with its thatch-like roof richly ornamented with simulated protective cover and supported on posts and beams, is an elegant reconstruction of a simple village shrine. The Arjuna, presumably reproducing a square two-storey vihara vimana, is prophetic of the main line of Dravidian development: its ground floor breaks forward towards the west to form a porch, cell-bordered terraces surround the main chamber of its upper floor and the 'clerestory' which supports its octagonal 'cupola'.

The unfinished three-storey Dharmaraja ('righteous king') is the grandest of the vimana type: two halls and a solid octagonal cupola are superimposed over a miniature apadana with shallow porticos inset on three sides and projecting to form the entrance from the west. On each of the upper terraces there is room for circumambulation between the parapet cells and the central hall. The Bhima – an unfinished clerestory-lit hall – stands before the Dharmaraja in the traditional relationship of mandapa to prasada: reproduction of the structural forms represented in the early Buddhist reliefs (see 9, pages 28–29) could hardly be closer.

40 **Mahaballipuram, Shore Temple** view from sea with
enclosure entrance gate (gopura).

Two vimanas – one of three storeys, the other of four –
rise from among subsidiary shrines in a precinct with a
monumental gate (the first of a long line). Containing
a square inner sanctum (garbha-griha) with porch, each
vimana is articulated with pilasters recalling the timber

prasada or vimana was long sustained in the Dravidian south where the storeys were marked by open terraces bordered with cell-like pavilions.

The Pallavas set the example in their so-called
rathas hewn from the rock at Mahaballipuram.[39]
Carved from monoliths – and preceded by a series of
excavated temples – the rathas seem to have been the
earliest freestanding stone temples in Pallavan
domains. These were modelled on the traditional
monastic forms bequeathed by the Buddhists – the
shrine, the mandapa, the multi-storey vihara with
cells bordering the upper terraces, all adapted to the
accommodation of the Hindu deity – and carefully
imitate the timber structure of the prototypes, with
the inclusion of brackets, joists, rafters and beams

prototype, like the rathas, though the rhythm is somewhat
irregular. Columns rise improbably from rearing lions, and a
lotus moulding is incorporated with the structurally derived
ones of the base. As no attempt was made to impose the
logic of timber structure on the plan, the vimanas' profile
is markedly steeper than that of the Dharmaraja Ratha.
Elegance seems to have been preferred to monumentality,
and the ornamental detail is comparatively rich.

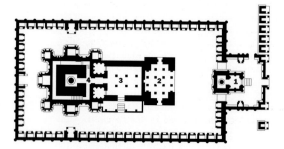

41 **Kanchipuram, Kailasanatha** founded by Rajasimha
towards the end of his reign and furthered by his successor,
Mahendra-varman III, c. 720–28, plan.

(1) Entrance gate (gopura) into main cell-bordered
compound; (2) original detached hall; (3) later link hall;
(4) vimana.

hardly required in stone and certainly not in monolithic sculpture.

The example of the rathas carved from rock was to
be followed elsewhere in India, not least at Ellora (see
44, pages 118–19). However, at Mahaballipuram excavation was superseded by construction early in the 8th
century for the Shore Temple[40] (probably founded by
Narasimha-varman II Rajasimha, c. 690–728).

The tradition was further developed at Kanchipuram, capital of the Pallavas, where the later great
works are even richer than the Shore Temple but also
more regular and monumental. In the Kailasanatha[41]
a simplified version of the Arjuna Ratha at Mahaballipuram serves for the Shiva shrines which back on to
the enclosure wall of the temple. In contrast, elongated roofs developing the Bhima form cover the
more substantial shrines on the main axes of the
vimana and the portals, which develop the gopura
prototype of the Shore Temple. Nine subsidiary
shrines are integrated with the main vimana – two
flanking the western entrance, seven equally spaced
on the other three sides – and a hall, originally
detached, was later joined to it.

The Vaikunthaperumal at Kanchipuram[42] has only

42 **Kanchipuram, Vaikunthaperumal** probably founded by Parameshvara-varman II, c. 728–31 and completed by Nandi-varman II, c. 731–96, section.

an attached hall and is set within a colonnaded cloister. In both this temple and the Kailasanatha, the vimana has four storeys, like the main one of the Shore Temple, but due to the inclusion of an inner ambulatory (doubled in the Vaikunthaperumal) the pyramidal gradation is even more broadly based than in the Dharmaraja Ratha.

Temples of the Deccan
These monumental and elegant structures provided models to be emulated by the Pallavas' neighbouring adversaries: the Chalukyas imported Pallavan craftsmen to produce their greatest works at Pattadakal.

According to inscriptions, the Virupaksha Temple at Pattadakal[43] was founded by the Chalukyan king Vikramaditya II (733–44) to commemorate his victory over the Pallavas. It marks the culmination of a series of temples in the southern style built at the Chalukyan political and ceremonial centres (Badami and Pattadakal respectively). Having occupied the Pallavan capital, Kanchipuram, Vikramaditya left an inscription in the Kailasanatha's hall recording his admiration for the architecture of his adversaries. Another inscription at Pattadakal records the importation of Pallavan craftsmen to work on the Virupaksha.

Pattadakal, in turn, inspired the excavation of the Kailasa Temple at Ellora for the Rashtrakutas.[44] Usually attributed to King Krishna I (756–75), whose predecessor's work on the neighbouring Dashavatara is recorded in inscriptions, this stupendous exercise

43 **Pattadakal, Virupaksha Temple** interior of the hall to the sanctum.

As in the Vaikunthaperumal at Kanchipuram, the attached hall and vimana are linked by a vestibule, but there is a detached pavilion for Shiva's bull, Nandi, in a more expansive compound. Padma-kumbha pilasters are the norm outside, but great square piers, occasionally relieved with bands and medallions as here, are the basic means of internal support, as in earlier Chalukyan works like the 'Durga Temple' at Aihole (see 37, page 100).

Outside, the concern with relief and a more even gradation of tiers was furthered by the imported Pallavan architects. The vigorous monumentality of the later Pallavan works, deriving from a clearly defined pyramidal form and the crisp delineation of carefully attuned parts, is fully realised in the four-storey Virupaksha.

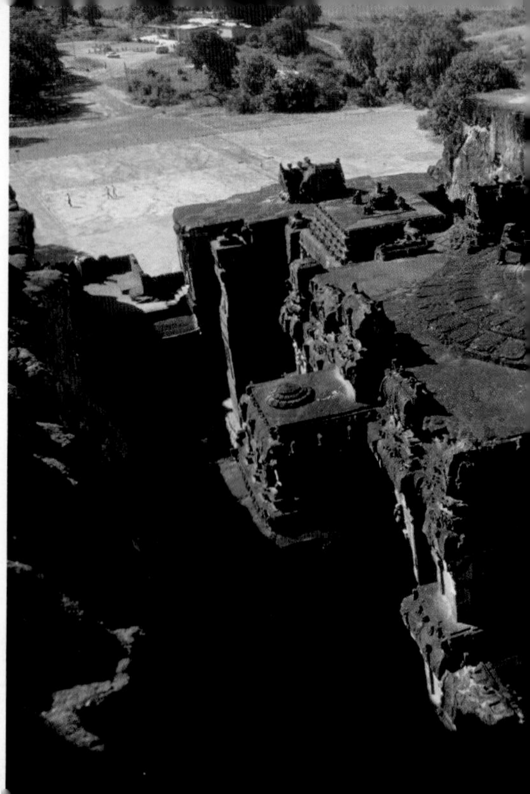

bears enough resemblance to the great Chalukyan works at Pattadakal and their models to suggest the involvement of southerners again.

The apogee of the tradition was achieved by the Chola king Rajaraja the Great in the Rajarajeshvara at Tanjavur,[45] whose 16-storey vimana was built to mark the expansion of the kingdom they inherited from the Pallavas into a great empire.

44 PREVIOUS PAGES **Ellora, Kailasa Temple** view from the east.

The Kailasa is a walled complex with a ceremonial gate. The principal axis leads through the forecourt, with the pavilion for Shiva's Nandi at its centre, to a nine-square hall with porch and balconies and a vestibule leading to the inner sanctum. This last, with its superstructure of three cell-bordered terraces and an octagonal cupola, is flanked by subsidiary shrines beyond an open ambulatory – as in the multi-storey vihara which provided the prototype for the southern vimana. The base mouldings, like the pillars of the hall, conform to the types encountered at Pattadakal. Subsidiary halls and shrines are excavated from the rock walls.

45 OVERLEAF **Tanjavur, Rajarajeshvara** c. 1010, detail of the vimana.

The towering masterpiece of a great line of Chola works, the majestic vimana here rises as a hollow pyramid to more than 63 metres (207 feet) through 16 storeys. The whole is crowned by a monolithic circular cupola – the method of raising these huge weights to such a height is the subject of continuing speculation. The intermediate storeys – the first four extending over the vestibule – bear various miniature shrine forms whose scale is calculated to provide relief without denying homogeneity.

The vimana encloses circumambulatory passages, unlike most early Chola works, but like the greatest works of the Pallavas which provided the obvious precedents for imperial pretension. Expressing the superimposition of these ambulatories around the immense linga, the first floor is divided into two registers separated by a full entablature. There are 11 bays, of which four have ceremonial pillars, and represent the base plane of the wall, while six have aedicules, and project between pilasters, the central pair of which are linked into a triad by a continuous entablature over the great voids which light the ambulatory wall and its superb icons.

The vestibule, similarly articulated but with entrances

to its sides as well as on axis with the inner sanctum, forms an intermediate element between the vimana and the imposing closed hall, once of three storeys with a later portico and a detached Nandi pavilion. All the contiguous elements share a common base and platform. The platform, projecting beyond the base, is vigorously indented throughout below an eave-like cornice (kapota) and frieze; the former is of the most elaborate type developed by the Cholas, combining two recessed friezes, the lower one with vyalas (lions or leopards), torus (kumuda) and minor cyma-recta mouldings.

Two main enclosures protect the vimana. The outer enclosure is surrounded by a moat and later defence works integrated with the magnificent five-storey ceremonial gate of Kulottunga III (1178–1218). The three-storey inner gateway on the same axis provides access to the main temple precinct through the inner enclosure wall; subsidiary gates to the north, south and west are aligned with the centre of the inner sanctum. Around the inner face of the enclosure, multiple subsidiary shrines – including one for the shakti, an essential element of the Chola temple – are sheltered by superimposed colonnades.

Northern temples

In the north progressively more abstract permutations of the prasada prototype gave rise to the main varieties of northern forms (called shikhara) which reflect the imagery of the mountain – the many-peaked Meru, Kailasa or Vaikuntha encountered in the shastras from the earliest reference to the superstructure of temples. The northern shikhara may be essentially a single entity (called latina) or it may be a cluster of spire-like forms (sekhari or bhumija). And, of course, diversification of mass responded to the increasingly complex system of projections produced by five centuries of development in plan.

The latina type has miniature blind lunettes in tiers marked by amalakas on the corners, and central bands (lata) of miniature lunettes in a mesh-like pattern over the main projections to the cella. Putative examples are to be found among experimental works across northern India, or at Osia,[46] but the form was to be taken to its apogee in the 11th century by the Somavamshis in Orissa, with the superimposition of miniature shikharas between the bands of blind lunettes: the Lingaraj at Bhubaneshwar is their masterpiece.[47] The most magnificent surviving example of

46 Osia, Surya Temple I.

The main works at Osian (near Jodhpur in modern Rajasthan) are the three so-called Hari-Hara temples, two Surya, two Shiva and two Vishnu shrines, the Pipla Matha and the Mahavira, the latter dated in a later inscription to the reign of the Pratihara king Vatsaraja (c. 777–808). In the absence of firm evidence the other works are generally ascribed to the same king and his immediate predecessors or successors: most have five-bay mulaprasadas, porch and open hall, but no vestibule or ambulatory.

47 **Bhubaneshwar, Lingaraj Temple** credited most
convincingly to Yayati II (c. 1020–40), view from the north.

Rising from a plethora of lesser shrines in a vast
compound, the majestic superstructure of the great Lingaraj
dominates the town. It represents the full maturity of the
Orissan tradition which dates back to the 7th century.
Then, in the Parashurameshvara in particular, there was
no developed relationship between hall and cella and the
complex variations in plane of the shikhara were not
reflected in the walls below. Following the precedent
set in the earliest mature works at Bhubaneshwar, the
Mukteshvara in particular, all the elements are co-ordinated
in the Lingaraj. The base has five tiers, one following the
profile of a water pot, as in the earlier work, and the five
bays of the cella are reflected in the shikhara. The greater
scale of the Lingaraj required two registers in the walls,
with miniature slab-roofed shrine forms providing niches
for the splendid icons.

The curve of the Lingaraj shikhara effected the canonical
latina balance between strength and grace: there are
miniature shikharas over the vestibule and in the
intermediate zones, where they are superimposed all the
way from the first storey to the last, enlivening the great
bulk most effectively. Elaborate kirtimukha gables with

the latina temple is the mid-11th-century Udayesh-vara[48] built by the Paramara king Udayaditya at his capital, Udayapur. The contemporary Ambaranatha at Ambarnath is another fine example of the type.[49]

The bhumija form has multiple corners, star-shaped or aligned diagonally, supporting tiers of miniature shikhara or shrine forms between the central projections and their strongly emphasised vertical bands of enmeshed lunettes. The sekhari type has one or more levels of graded miniature shikharas in the diagonals, and half and quarter ones with niches above the central and intermediate projections to the cella walls. The culmination of a gradual process first detected (in

lion finials relieve the centres of its three outer faces above the blind doors and, as in all northern varieties, it is crowned by a massive amalaka, here supported by more heraldic lions. The progressively diminishing slabs of the hall roof, culminating in a double-lotus finial, are interrupted by the recessed vertical of a gallery. The lower slab interferes with the spring of the shikhara, suggesting to some that the hall was added later, like the subsidiary shrines at the cardinals of the cella and the pavilions for ritual dancing and feasting beyond it.

so far as the accidents of survival allow) at
Gyaraspur,[50] the works of the Solankis at Modhera
and the Chandellas at Khajuraho are the supreme sur-
vivors of the type.

The main series of temples at Khajuraho begins with
the Lakshmana, the Vaishnavite foundation of King

48 OVERLEAF **Udayapur, Udayeshvara Temple** inscribed
by its founder 1059, view from the south.

The seven-bay cella and nine-square closed hall stand
on a platform facing east and are surrounded by seven
subsidiary shrines. The bays of the cella, amplified for the
hall, radiate like the points of a star within a circle. The
facets are treated as piers bearing aedicules, and diminutive
piers support substantial model shikharas in the seven-tiered
superstructure between the delicately incised bands of
meshed miniature niches which face the cardinal directions.

The base is comparable to the fully developed type found
on 11th-century works in the domains of the Solankis and
their neighbours. Below the floor slab, the early form of
socle consisting of kalasha and karnaka on a thick slab
(called kumbha because of its rounded shoulder) is raised to
form a dado above major and minor padmas and karnakas
superimposed over several more slabs.

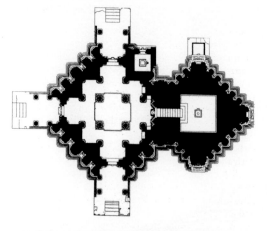

49 Ambarnath, Ambaranatha Temple inscribed
c. 1060, plan.

Unlike in the contemporary work at Udayapur (see 48, pages 130–31), the rectangular faceting at Ambarnath produced squares joined on their diagonals. Instead of diminutive piers and substantial model shikharas in the superstructure, substantial piers support tiny shrines, and the base is richer in its decorative detail.

Yashovarman I (died c. 950), continues with the Shivite Vishvanatha of Dhanga (c. 950–1002), the Surya Chitragupta and Vaishnavite Jagadamba of Ganda (1002–17), and concludes with the Shivite Khandariya of Vidyadhara (1017–29).[51-52] The Lakshmana, Vishvanatha and Khandariya have an enclosed ambulatory around the inner sanctum and an open pavilion between the portico and closed hall, unlike the Chitragupta and Jagadamba. All have high, broad and elaborately moulded platforms, that of the Khandariya joined to the Jagadamba's to provide for the small Mahadevi. All have high and elaborate socles and dados incorporating the full range of water-pot, lotus and astragal mouldings over superimposed slabs and an increasing number of friezes. The Lakshmana has walls of two registers and five bays, the others three registers and seven bays. The principal manifestations of the deity in their blind doors, visible from without in the central projections of the Chitragupta and Jagadamba, are lit by the balconies opening from the ambulatories of the other three great works.

A discernible progression confirms the inscriptional evidence for their dating. Like the second generation of sekhari works in the Pratihara period, after

50 Gyaraspur, Mala Devi Temple datable from
inscriptions to the late 9th century, view from below.

Partly excavated, the plan is relatively advanced among
works from the Pratihara period: there is an ambulatory
as well as a vestibule and a closed hall made cruciform by
balconies and porch. The shikhara has nine miniature latina
forms clustered about its base. The roofs of both hall and
porch are in the form of a stepped pyramid (phamsana).

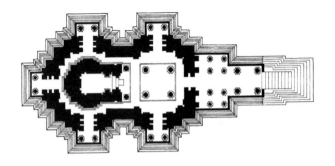

51 Khajuraho, Khandariya Temple inscribed by the
Chandella king Vidyadhara (1017–29), plan.

**52 OVERLEAF Khajuraho, Khandariya, Mahadevi and
Jagadamba Temples** view from the south-east.

The progression in the Khandariya's masses to their
climax, the contrast between solid and void, the tension
between horizontal and vertical, resolved in the
monumental but elegant composition of the shikhara
through the agency of small-scale but comprehensible forms
reflecting the whole of which they are parts, make this work
one of the supreme achievements of Indian architecture.

Gyaraspur, the shikharas of the Lakshmana and the two smaller temples have only two levels of minor spirelets and one major spirelet to each projection. The shikhara of the Vishvanatha is hardly more complex but the build-up of the series of masses from the portico to their climax in it is much more resoundingly orchestrated. In this it set a crucial precedent for the Khandariya, but the superstructure over each of the elements in that latest work is far more complex: the slabs of the earlier hall roofs have given way to minia-

53 **Khajuraho, Khandariya Temple** detail.

In addition to the cult of their orthodox dedicatees, most of the Khajuraho temples seem also to have been associated with heterodox tantric sects. Their walls are alive with wonderful shardulas, apsaras and mithunas whose vigorous sexuality reflects the elaboration of the *Kama Sutra*. Below the walls and the floor slab is the dado of karnaka, kalasha and kumbha. Below the dado, the base exceeds the most elaborate of its predecessors amongst the northern schools: in addition to the full range of padma, astragal and kumbha mouldings, together with numerous slabs, it includes friezes of sacrificial animals, symbolic beasts and narratives relevant to the patron.

ture shrines, and the shikhara is unprecedentedly tall and slender, with no less than four half-spires before each of its central projections.

The Solanki and Chandella schools are specially notable for elaboration – of bases and walls as well as superstructure – and their sculpture is correspondingly prolix. Apart from the great icons in the blind doors, attendant in the proliferation of niches (rathikas) are myriad yogini, cosmic power and its stimulation being represented as the virile leogryph (sardula), the indolent damsel (alasa-kanya), the dance of celestial apsaras and the salvation (mukti) to which it is all directed, the new birth of salvation as release – mithuna.[53]

Synthesis and elaboration

The northern and southern traditions were cross-fertilised by the Later Chalukyas in west-central India in a synthesis of palace and mountain imagery that reflects attitudes of mind as ancient as the mystical identification of Indra's yashti with the *axis mundi*, with the cosmic mountain Meru, and of Meru itself with the prasada of the gods. The vimana retained its essentially southern storeyed form but the definition

of the architectonic parapet elements decreased as pla-
nar variation increased to a climax in the centre, as in
the Kashivishveshvara of Lakkundi.[54] This tradition
was enriched by the Hoysalas in southern Deccan with
star-shaped plans inspired by the bhumija form. The
most complete example is the Keshava Temple at Somnathpur with its dazzling triple vimanas preceded by
closed and open halls.[55–56]

As at Somnathpur, the Hoysalas were fond of multi-
shrined complexes and star-shaped plans – like the
northern Deccanis and Malwans. Characteristic of the
school are tiered platforms echoing the perimeter of
the buildings they support, superimposed frieze slabs
in the base, screened halls, columns that seem to have
been turned on a lathe, bold figural brackets and profuse ornamentation carved like ivory or sandalwood.

All northern and central temples had substantial
halls, usually based on nine squares in plan. The closed
form of hall usually matches the cella – though amplified – and they sit on either side of porches or balconies
which are invariably bordered by low parapets supporting a seat-like ledge with vertical or sloping back,
truncated columns and deeply projecting eaves. Early
pillars were usually square, often with vertical or

54 **Lakkundi, Kashivishveshvara Temple** inscribed in
1087 but possibly subsequently rebuilt in part, detail of
the vimana.

After a century of effort, the maturity of the Later
Chalukyan style had been achieved by the end of the
11th century at several Deccani sites including Hangal,
Kuruvatti, Ittagi and Lakkundi. The walls of cella and
closed hall have greater plasticity than in the earlier works
of the school (at Kukkanur, for example) due both to
the enhanced depth of projection and to the consistent
interpolation of piers in the peripheral recessions. The
various constituent elements of the southern vimana have
resolved themselves into a series of luxurious horizontal
mouldings which step forward more vigorously than in
the earlier works, and as plasticity increased, definition of
the architectonic parapet elements decreased. Somewhat
ironically, however, structural forms reassert themselves as
miniature vimanas or shikharas over the pier buttresses of
the intermediate recessions and as pediments to the blind
doors. The central dormers quite eclipse the cells from
which they are elaborated and the interpenetration of
horizontals and verticals is complete at Lakkundi, where the
miniature sekhari shikharas over the blind doors actually
break through the entablature.

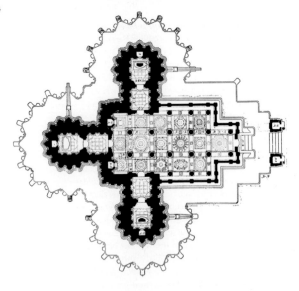

55 **Somnathpur, Keshava Temple** datable from an inscription of 1268, plan of triple shrine.

horizontal projections (see 43, page 117), but later elaboration superimposed polygonal and circular zones treated to rich relief, below a variety of capitals including the 'bowl of plenty' (purna-kalasha).[57] Corbelled arches, either undulating or cusped, are thrown between columns. Arches over doors, windows or niches, once of bowed bamboo, assumed the form of the makara, while the horseshoe dormer became

56 OVERLEAF **Somnathpur, Keshava Temple** view from the south-east.

Small but still virtually intact, the triple-shrine Keshava is set in a compound surrounded by an enclosure with cloisters sheltering 64 subsidiary shrines. The star-shaped vimanas share a nine-square pavilion, extended to provide entrance hall and porch. The facets of the walls have lavish icons below valanced eaves and aedicules crowned with miniature vimanas. The superstructures, with four parapets of vestigial cells, reflect every variation of plane in the walls below.

The columns of porch and hall are mainly of the 'lathe-turned' type, with and without fluting across the mouldings, and the ceiling compartments are distinguished by a stunning diversity of pattern.

57 **Ittagi, Mahadeva Temple** inscribed in 1112, open hall.

In addition to the usual sequence of cella, vestibule and nine-square hall, many Later Chalukyan temples have magnificent cruciform open halls with equilateral projections between the arms of the cross, and sumptuous ceilings. Fertility of invention in varying the form of the column – many apparently turned on a lathe, some fluted across all the mouldings – is nowhere better displayed than here at Ittagi.

the gaping leonine monster kirtimukha, symbol of eclipse – the cosmic sexual act from which existence is reborn. In place of the early flat roof, the mature works usually had pyramids of stepped slabs, called phamsana (see 47, page 126), or tiers of miniature bell-shaped lotus forms, called samvarana (see 42, page 114). Ceilings were first flat, but elaborate corbelling later produced dazzling compositions with receding courses of lotiform cusps and matching central pendants borne on flying figural brackets (see 60, page 154).

Jaina shrines

In northern India the indigenous civilisation was devastated from the end of the 11th century as the Muslims established permanent domains there – at first the Delhi Sultanate, then independent kingdoms on the basis of former Hindu ones. The Hindu tradition was suppressed, if not extinguished. However, the Jains sustained their exceptionally rich permutation of it in the mountain fastnesses of Kathiawar and

58 OVERLEAF **Ranakpur, Dharana-Vihara** view from the south-west.

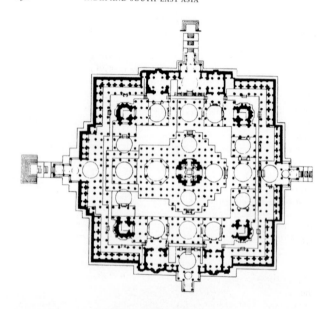

59 **Ranakpur, Dharana-Vihara** mid 15th century, plan.

Gujarat, and in neighbouring Rajasthan, in the replacement or supplement of earlier shrines desecrated by the Muslims.

Ministers of the Solanki rulers provided patronage for the great series of Jaina shrines at Mount Abu in Gujarat, inaugurated in the 11th century but not completed for 200 years, and the extraordinary achievement echoed through the rugged mountain ranges of the west. As elsewhere in India, the Jains drew directly on the Hindu repertory of forms, reorganising them to cater for their devotion to multiple tirthankaras ('ford makers'). As in the typical orthodox Hindu shrine of the region, the main elements are a cella with ambulatory preceded by closed and open halls aligned east–west on a platform. But the Jaina works are distinguished from their Brahmanical counterparts by the extremely rich Jaina iconography, and their most characteristic feature – anticipated in the typical Buddhist sanctuary – is the row of miniature cellas introduced to house repeated images of all the tirthankaras on the edge of the platform and framing a court in front of the main shrine. A sumptuous open hall of nine squares was usually inserted into the court.

The culmination was the four-faced (chaturmukha)

60 **Ranakpur, Dharana-Vihara** view through the great hall beyond the western entrance to the four-square complex.

Dedicated to Adinatha, the first of the 24 Jaina tirthankaras ('ford makers' for the 'Way of the Conqueror'), this stupendous building represents the final flowering of the Solanki tradition in north-west India.

Literary references to the form date from the 12th century and the Dharana-Vihara at Ranakpur was supposedly modelled on vanished 12th-century Solanki prototypes. It has no closed hall but a three-storey open hall stands before each face of the cella, the one to the west being the most majestic. Beyond these, additional triple-height halls communicate with the entrance halls, and yet more serve subsidiary shrines in the corners.

The view from the entrance through the western halls, with a beam of sunlight entering their clerestories and penetrating the suffused atmosphere to illuminate a succession of individual elements on the shafts of the many-faceted piers, is unsurpassed in all India.

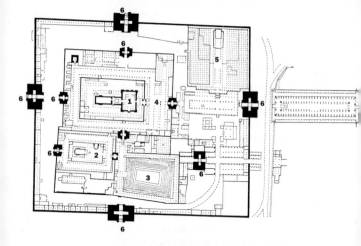

61 **Madurai, Minakshi-Sundareshvara** plan.
(1) Sundareshvara (Shiva) shrine; (2) Minakshi (shakti)
shrine; (3) tank; (4) Viravasantaraya mandapa with
Nandi statue; (5) 'thousand-pillared' Airakkal mandapa;
(6) gatehouses; (7) entrance hall of the 18th-century ruler
Tirumalai Nayak.

temple with multi-storey halls succeeding one another before all four sides of a cella enshrining a four-faced image of the Jina ('Conqueror'). The earliest surviving example is the Dharana-Vihara at Ranakpur.[58-59] Indirectly lit, infused by the opalescent sheen of the local Arasa marble, the open hall beyond the western entrance is the chief glory of Jaina architecture.[60]

Southern temple cities

In southern India the indigenous tradition went on unbroken, despite Muslim pretensions, and the temple continued to develop as the centre of the way of life of the community as a whole, along the lines stated in the Rajarajeshvara at Tanjavur (see 45, page 122). Expanded over many generations, the Chola complex set the pattern followed by the rulers of Vijayanagar and their nayaka successors until the 17th century and beyond in the development of the great 'temple cities' which still dominate the land of the Tamils.

Patronage of temples flagged with the decline of the Cholas, and the Pandyas did little more than add to

62 OVERLEAF **Madurai, Minakshi-Sundareshvara** view from the southern gatehouse.

existing sanctuaries – not least the Minakshi complex in Madurai,[61-62] their capital, after it was devastated by the Muslims in 1310. Even if a venerable shrine was not susceptible to aggrandisement, its environment was: Vijayanagaran rulers and their successors competed in the acquisition of merit through the provision of additional compounds with ever more dominant (if increasingly less architectonic) gatehouses, and a wide range of facilities related to one another with varying degrees of regularity.

Thus at most of the major southern cult centres, enclosure after enclosure ringed the original shrine, providing for the temple's expanding role in the life of the community, with facilities ranging from ablution tanks to teaching halls and, above all, to cater for developing cults like those of Shiva Nataraja and Devi, the shakti of the deity. Linked by cavernous colonnades,[63] there were extraordinary pillared halls for regular rituals, periodic festivals and occasional cultural performances; also accommodation for priests, sect gurus, attendant Brahmins and all the other temple officers and servants from ritual specialists to cleaners, and dormitories, refectories and infirmaries for pilgrims.

63 **Tiruchirapalli (Srirangam Island), Jambukeshvara Temple** 16th-century colonnaded gallery.

While the main temple hall was usually on axis with the principal shrine, others were provided as space permitted in existing or specially built enclosures. In addition to mandapas, great galleries surround interior courts and link them to other major elements in the complex, the ablution tank in particular. The elaboration of piers, columns, capitals and brackets was increasingly anti-architectonic: above all, Vijayanagaran builders and their followers delighted in attaching highly involved sculpture groups, usually including rampant beasts, to multi-faceted shafts.

The gatehouse – which emerged in the early Pallavan works and attained monumentality under the greatest of the Cholas – became the most prominent feature of the southern temple-city. It began to overshadow the vimana under the later Cholas and ultimately dominated not merely the temple compound but the entire surrounding countryside. Generally the first two storeys are of stone, the second continuing in the plane of the first, and the diminishing tiers of the superstructure are of plastered brick – the material facilitating decorative exuberance.

At first essentially architectonic in articulation, like the vimana, the structure of the gatehouses was obscured in later Vijayanagaran works by profuse fig-ure sculpture. Under the nayakas the structure was totally eclipsed and the profile was given an elegant concave curve. This is well illustrated by the series of monumental gates in the great Minakshi-Sundaresh-vara at Madurai, the most celebrated of all the south-ern temple-cities (see 62, pages 158–59). The stupendous series of 21 gatehouses at Srirangam spans the whole period: had it been completed, the latest would have risen to some 90 metres (295 feet) – twice the height of the outermost southern one at Madurai.

The remains and descriptions of earliest Madurai, the capital of the Pandyan kingdom from ancient times, together with the descriptions of cities like Ayodhya, Mathura and Indraprashtra (Delhi) make it clear that early Indian town planning conformed to the principles of order conveyed in the Vedic treatises for laying out a sacred site (see 6, page 19). The most potent surviving witnesses to this are the great temple cities of the south, not least the Madurai Minakshi complex itself (see 62, pages 158–59).

Planning and fortification

In the *Arthashastra*, the treatise on statecraft attributed to Chandragupta Maurya's chancellor Kautilya, planning for the fortified metropolis – there is no distinction in principle between camp, village and town and all would have been fortified – starts with a ring road corresponding to the ambulatory route around sacred sites. While the walled perimeter would conform to the location in practice, the ideal was rectangular – like that of the Romans. Aligned with the four cardinal points, two major axial roads and parallel subsidiary streets divided the town into wards graded for the different castes into which Indian society was divided. The gods were installed at the central cross-ing, the king to its north. Called the inner town, the king's walled complex of courts and pavilions (man-dapas and prasadas) was not unlike that of the gods.

Kautilya calls for defence in depth: ramparts of im-pacted mud dug from several ditches, preceded by an open field of fire (maidan) and crowned with several ring-walls. There were to be roofed walks wide enough for passing patrols and regularly spaced towers. Gates between twin towers, large enough for elephants, opened the main axes. Each was preceded by a draw-bridge spanning the ditches – at least one of which was to be flooded – and an assailant was to be thwarted by a wide range of obstacles, including tortuous deflec-tion of the line of approach. Several reliefs from the

64 Sanchi, relief from the Great Stupa.

Typically, a ceremonial portal (torana) in an outer palisade precedes a drawbridge which leads to a twin-towered galleried gatehouse in a massive wall. Crenellation, embrasures for marksmen and battering were characteristic and the projection of the gate tower's upper storeys may have accommodated elementary machicolation. Within these defence works are clustered several prasadas.

gates of the Great Stupa at Sanchi[64] provide a clear
general view of the early Indian metropolis which is
not inconsistent in detail with Kautilya's prescriptions.

Relying for security on the ingenuity of man, the
metropolitan fort is one of six types distinguished by
Kautilya in accordance with the nature of the site.
Strategy overruled tactics in the siting of most urban
complexes in open country, but forts were well isolated
by tracts of forest, desert, marsh or water and, of
course, best perched on precipitous outcrops of rock
as the acropolis of a town. On all these types of site,
up and down the subcontinent, the ruins of citadels
built to protect once palatial apartments bear testi-
mony to the conservatism of the Indian tradition – and
to the passion of the Indian ruler for change.

Chittor

Even among India's unexcelled range of spectacular
forts, none is better than Chittor.[65] The principal
ascent to the acropolis, nearly 200 metres (656 feet)
above the plain, is from the west, but there are subsidiary paths to the north and east. These have one and
four gates respectively, including the major eastern
Suraj Pol. Across the sinuous western approach, a

series of seven massive gates leads to the Ram Pol. All except the first of these have twin towers, and in most the lower masonry is comparable with 11th-century Hindu work elsewhere on the site, though the battlements seem generally to have been rebuilt later – prob-

65 OVERLEAF **Chittor fort** view from the south-west with the Tower of Victory right of centre and the Palace of Rana Kumbha on the edge of the ramparts left of centre.

Supposedly called after its founder, Chitrangad Maurya, Chitrakuta is mentioned first in the 7th century. A century later it had passed to the Guhilots and then successively to the Pratiharas, Rashtrakutas and Paramaras before returning to the Guhilots in the 11th century. They soon acknowledged the sovereignty of the Solankis and, with them, Chittor fell to the Delhi Sultan, Ala-ud-din Khalji, in 1303. With the Sultanate in disarray in the mid 14th century, the Sisodia Guhilots expelled the Muslims and refounded Chittor as a main centre of Rajput power.

There is no record of massive damage to the walls, beyond the breaches made by Mughal artillery in the 16th century, and the walls of Chittor are generally considered to be the finest examples of feudal Hindu defence works to survive in any degree of completeness.

ably after the assaults of the early 14th century. The fourth and fifth gates were rebuilt with arches, but all the rest have lintels carried on corbel brackets in the Hindu manner, with varying degrees of elaboration culminating in the sumptuous 15th-century Ram Pol. This has a richly moulded base incorporating three friezes like those of temples built immediately before the Muslim invasion. There are no barbicans, but a portico with elaborately carved columns provides shelter for the guard commanding the entrance.

To prevent circumvention, cross walls link the second, fourth, fifth and sixth gates to the main ramparts which ring the summit over the precipitous slopes. The mural battlements, like those of the gates, are distinct from post-Muslim work elsewhere. The bastions are slightly battered and the merlons have a 'pointed-arch' profile – which might suggest Muslim influence on restoration work – but the embrasures splay out from narrow slits below a continuous string course.

When Chittor was first occupied is uncertain but, as the key to Rajasthan, it must always have been the objective of any would-be potentate there.

Passion for change, and war, of course, have meant that invariably little remains of the fort palaces built before the Muslims achieved predominance in India – indeed even for a considerable time thereafter. It is evident that one or other of the ancient native and imported types – the prasada, the mandapa or apadana, the iwan – still always dominates, but for well over a millennium following the fall of Parthian Sirkap in the 1st century AD, tracing the course of secular developments involves conjecture.

Development of the native tradition

The native tradition, taken to its apogee by the imperial rulers of Vijayanagar in the 16th century, survived intact in the south at least until the end of the 18th century, when the Nyaka of Tanjavur reproduced its prasadas and mandapas in coarse masonry and with intrusive arcading.[66] Naturally, the Muslims asserted foreign forms, even in their relatively limited holdings in the south, but the traditions of the Persians and the Parthians can hardly have been forgotten in the north. It seems improbable that the imperial Kushanas did not lend lasting prestige to the iwan of their lesser predecessors: equally improbable that,

66 **Tanjavur, Nyaka's palace** c. 1800.
    The substitution of coarse masonry for timber apart,
the native tradition of prasada and attached mandapa is
compromised only by the intrusion of arcading in the latter.

bent on reviving the imperium of their greatest predecessors, the Gupta failed to emulate the apadana of
Chandragupta Maurya's Pataliputra – itself an ampli-
fication of the native mandapa.

The earliest palace built for a Hindu ruler of which
much substance survives is the Palace of Rana
Kumbha at Chittor of 1433–68.[67] Beyond the gate,
the mandapa of public audience and the prasada-like
residential blocks clearly assert their integrity, though
they are attached to the walls of courts in which
the imported idea of the iwan is translated with trabeated terms into mandapa-like recessions to the
ground floor.

Fifty years later, the synthesis of all the elements,
native and imported, is complete in the Palace of Man
Singh in the great fort at Gwalior.[68] The splendid ramparts and Hathi Pol (elephant gate) are clearly in direct
line of descent from those at Sanchi (see 64, page 167) but
the prasadas have become elaborate chattris on the
towers. Within, the main halls are represented as mandapas in the native trabeated mode, though they are
formally integrated with walled courts in accordance
with the imported tradition of the iwan. On the principal level of the royal apartments the halls and cham-

67 **Chittor fort, Palace of Rana Kumbha** 1433–68, Tripolia Gate with the court and audience hall beyond.

Terminating the series of gates along the ascent to the acropolis, the principal entrance to Rana Kumbha's palace compound, guarded by twin octagonal towers, is embellished with serpentine brackets between post and beam in the Hindu manner and with niches in the form of the Islamic arch. Within is an elongated trabeated portico for the guard, the right-hand range aligned with the audience mandapa. Beyond this open public zone, in the seemingly random distribution of rooms around private courts, there is no obvious distinction between the ruler's personal quarters and the accommodation of the royal women. However, relatively formal elements may be distinguished: on the south-western corner of the main building, opposite the Tripolia, the tower rises over doubled halls which address the main inner court in the manner of iwans; adjacent to another tower on the north-west corner, beyond the innermost court, is a three-storey block with a rectangular hall flanked by a pair of square chambers. Hardly less than the towers themselves, this latter structure is distinct, and all three elements, with their superimposed balconies carried on elaborate brackets and piers, recall the prasada.

bers are formally disposed about two square courts,[69-70] though these are not axially aligned. All these spaces are essentially human in scale, despite external appearances, and as richly varied in volume as in surface ornament. The zenana (harem) quarters above have communication passages to the outside and roof terraces with pavilions, and overlook the courts from screened galleries between deep eaves. Subterranean chambers recall the subterranean rooms

68 PREVIOUS PAGES **Gwalior fort with Palace of Man Singh** 1486–1516, ramparts and Hathi Pol from the south.

High on the edge of the vast spur which dominates the town, access to Man Singh's palace is gained by a typically tortuous route through a series of gates culminating in the precinct portal – as Kautiliya required. The walls retain rich blue, white and yellow tilework in the context of a sumptuous articulation incorporating elements drawn from both the native trabeated and imported arcuated traditions, carved in relatively high relief from fine masonry. The private apartments are within the walls adjacent to the gate; the range with galleries and two-storey chattris borders the main audience (durbar) court. Beyond are four palaces of later rulers.

69 **Gwalior, Palace of Man Singh** main eastern court of
the private apartments.

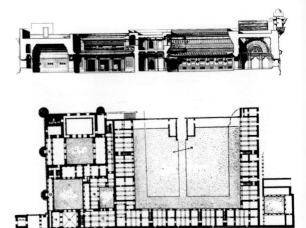

70 **Gwalior, Palace of Man Singh** east–west section and plan.

The structure is a traditional trabeated one, the eaves and galleries supported on particularly luxurious serpentine brackets, the piers which screen the main spaces from the (serdabs) long provided in Persian and Mesopotamian palaces for summer retreat.

Datia and Jodhpur

The Chittor and Gwalior palaces stand at the head of an extensive series of important works, including the palaces built for 17th- and 18th-century Rajput rulers at Datia and Jodhpur. At Datia[71] a single great square court is surrounded by mandapa-like iwans and self-assertive prasada-like towers, but rising free in the centre is a truly monumental prasada containing the raja's apartments.[72] Linked to the sides by elegant bridges, the massive block is raised over subterranean rooms, hewn from the rock on which it is founded, and a continuous arcaded basement. The square court is framed by ranges of apartments on two levels, surrounded by external screened galleries and surmounted by terraces with eight pavilions – as in the

courts bearing capitals descended from the forms elaborated by the Chandellas and their contemporaries. The roofing of the main western hall was achieved pragmatically by laying large slabs of stone against a raised transom, but there is a false ribbed vault over the eastern chamber.

71 **Datia, Govind Mahal of Raja Bir Singh Deo**
1605–27, view from the south-west.

Jahangiri Mahal at nearby Orchha, built by the same ruler earlier in his reign.

The combination of stout traditional defences and Rajput palace building at its most convoluted is nowhere better represented than by the old fort at Jodhpur. Its eminence provides a commanding view of the surrounding desert, and the walls rising from the rocky face were unassailable. Multi-storey prasada-like blocks and mandapa-like iwans are wholly integrated into a complex of courts.[73] On all sides of the 17th-century ranges – and the 18th-century additions to their north – are multi-storey prasadas hung with galleries and balconies carried on extremely rich corbels. They are screened with a profusion of jalis, dazzling in their intricacy, which provide an outer skin to protect the living-spaces from the rigours of the desert climate.

The prasada-like blocks were rarely emulated, but the iwans set the pattern for endless elaboration until the ancient Indian tradition ceded to the ways of the west.

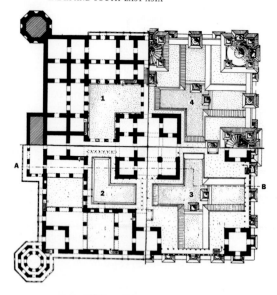

72 **Datia, Govind Mahal** quartered plan of the first four floors, ascending 1–4, and section.

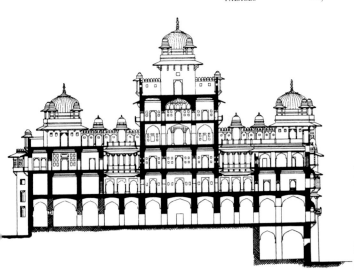

73 Jodhpur, Mothi Mahal of Raja Jaswant Singh (1638–78).

The steep approach to the fort is guarded by seven gates: beyond the top one it leads sideways to the main audience court. This is flanked by 17th-century buildings, including the Mothi Mahal to its south, but the nucleus of the complex dates back to the mid 15th century.

On the ground floor of the Mothi Mahal, to the west of its court, is the main hall of audience. Its size suggests a public role, its position a private one, but the lack of a clear distinction between public and private zones is not untypical of the Rajput palace.

The style of decoration, inside and out, is indebted to developments at the court of the Mughal Emperor Shah Jahan, which were themselves inspired by the indigenous traditions of Bengal and Gujarat.

74 **Parambanan, great temple complex** blind door with
kirtimukha lintel and brahmanical figure.

The great Mauryan king Ashoka (c. 272–232 BC) is reputed to have sent missionaries to convert Sri Lanka and Burma to Buddhism. These two countries on the periphery of India have been predominantly Buddhist ever since, though the faith has long been eclipsed by Hinduism and Islam in India itself.

Not long after Ashoka, Indian traders were taking Indian ideas to Indonesia. Travelling without wives, sailors and merchants settled and married there. The children were raised in the faith of their fathers – Buddhism at first, Hinduism from the middle of the first millennium AD. The religion of their mothers – and their native forebears – was animistic, and the synthesis of the two produced the extraordinary architecture of ancient Java.

Religions and dynasties

The first great kingdom in the Indonesian archipelago was Srivijaya, which controlled Sumatra from the 7th until the 13th century. It is, of course, on the prosperity brought by the exercise of determined authority over an extensive area that the production of monumental architecture to celebrate that authority depends. Extending its sway over Malaya, Borneo

and western Java and even the north coast of the
Gulf of Thailand, Srivijaya achieved the former but
not the latter – at least not in effecting the transition
from perishable native timber construction to
durable masonry. Eighth-century princes in the centre and east of Java, on the other hand, were spectacularly successful in laying the foundations for
monumentality.

The rulers of Srivijaya were Buddhist and so too
was the Sailendra dynasty which ruled eastern Java
from the mid 7th century. Their contemporaries in the
centre, the Sanjayas, were Hindu. As we have seen,
Brahmanism is a birthright which comes with inherited caste. Opposing this with its heterodox promise
of release from the inexorable cycle of existence, the
Mahayana is universal by nature: it proved as attrac-
tive to foreigners of all classes as it had to Indians. On
the other hand, while it is easy to see how a Hindu
population developed in Indian colonies abroad, it is
less easy to explain the rise of Hindu ruling classes
beyond those colonies. Of course, a ruler may merely
exercise his whim – whatever Brahmanical purists in
India might say – but it has been speculated that a
prince from the declining Gupta house escaped the

depredations of the Huns in the late 5th-century sub-continent by defying taboo and travelling over the sea in the wake of the merchants, taking brahmins with him. The first Sailendra, too, is reputed to have left Orissa in the mid 7th century and established himself in eastern Java as 'Lord of the Isles, King of the Mountain'.

The Sailendras and Sanjayas exhausted themselves in territorial rivalry, but seem to have merged through marriage around 850, just before the triumph of a prince from the east who founded the kingdom of Mataram. He claimed descent from the Sanjayas. The last of the Sailendras took refuge at the court of Srivijaya, which was suffering its own reverses, ulti-mately regained power there and sought to extend it back to Java. Mataram was restricted to the east of the island c. 927. It staged a comeback at the end of the century, was threatened with extinction in reprisal, but reached its apogee in the mid 11th cen-tury under the son of the last king's daughter and her Balinese consort.

Early in the 13th century, internecine rivalry pro-duced the Singasari dynasty who conquered Sumatra and even challenged China. Under threat of Chinese invasion, the Singasari were removed in a palace coup, but were revived by a pretender based on Mahjapahit in 1294. His was the last effective Hindu regime in Indonesia before the the final triumph of Islam in the 15th century.

The synthesis of Indian religious ideals and native animism in monuments of stone was achieved by the rival Buddhist Sailendras and Hindu Sanjayas. However they originally espoused their faiths, they and their courts (kratons) retained an essentially native mysticism, encouraging syncretism rather than a strict adherence to theological dogma. Their subjects were devoted to the spirits of their ancestors, including those of trees and water which the Buddha had been sage enough to woo in any case, and they themselves were overwhelmingly impressed by the great epics imported by the Indians, especially by the Ramayana's ideal of kingship, which achieved its apogee in Sri Rama's identification as an avatar of Vishnu. It is hardly surprising, therefore, that the principal building type of courtly Indo-Indonesia was the candi, a sepulchral monument for a deified king dedicated to the Buddha, Shiva or Vishnu.

The candi

Built over a square plan, the typical candi consists of a cubical cella, oriented to the cardinal directions, resting on a broad base providing for circumambulation, and surmounted by a pyramid of tiered terraces bordered by multiple miniature shrines – like the prasada-vimanas of the Pallavas (from the domains of whose predecessors the earliest Buddha images had come to Indonesia). The image of the patron deity was enshrined in the cella; the ashes of the deceased prince were encapsulated in a subterranean chamber.

The cella walls usually project to frame the entrance from the east and blind doors on the other three sides.[74] Often naga- (water spirit) or makara-toranas with a kirtimukha mask at the apex, these were readily understood by the natives as representing the spirits to which they were principally devoted, and the assimilation of imported forms was complete when images of the deified prince stood for the Buddhist, Shivite or Vaishnavite figures in the niches of the blind doors.

The oldest dated stone monument in Java is Candi Kalasan[75] on the Dieng plateau north of Merapi. Dedicated to the bodhisattva Tara in 778, it seems to have been the sepulchre of the wife of the first Sailendra ruler. As usual, sadly, the image has gone from the cella. However, the 9th-century Candi Mendut, which may not in fact have been a sepulchre, still preserves its splendid Buddha flanked by bodhisattvas.[76]

A square extends in plan to a Greek cross, each wing of which contains a square room entered though a kirtimukha portal, the eastern one alone forming a vestibule to the central square cella. Plinth and cornice mouldings are consistent throughout and the three-tiered superstructure rises to 21 metres (69 feet). Earlier, in the 8th century, buildings like Candi Bhima, also on the Dieng plateau, project only to a porch based on a plinth consistent with that of the cella but somewhat uncomfortably juxtaposed with the main mass at cornice level. Columns are avoided, though the structure is essentially trabeated, but like the earliest surviving examples in northern and central India, the superstructure relates directly to the prasada prototype,

75 **Dieng plateau, Candi Kalasan** 778, exterior.

The Dieng plateau below Mount Merapi, beyond the main centres of political power, was the resort of holy men whose hermitages and monasteries were the objects of pilgrimage and foci for burials.

with figures looking from rows of horseshoe-shaped dormer windows between amalaka finials at the corners. As in later works, such as Candi Kalasan, string courses assert the horizontals. Unlike them, the walls are unreleived with figure sculpture.

Javan candis vary in form and decoration, departing further from the Indian model towards the indigenous the further east they were conceived: given the two poles of indigenous inheritance and imported legacy, that is the mark of an essential conservatism. The grandest is central, though built for the eastern Mataram ruler c. 915. This is the richly embellished Shivite Lara Djonggrang at Parambanan, flanked by the smaller Brahma and Vishnu candis on a square, shrine-bordered terrace below the centre of which the ruler's ashes were incarcerated.[77-78]

The Great Stupa at Borobodur

If the complex at Parambanan is a candi, its three principal elements are Hindu temples, and similar, if smaller, shrines were widespread in Java. For their

76 **Dieng Plateau, Candi Mendut** 9th century, interior of the main cella with Buddha image.

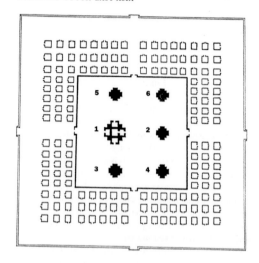

77 **Parambanan, great temple complex** c. 900,
plan.

(1) Shiva candi; (2) Nandi pavilion; (3) Brahma candi;
(4) pavilion; (5) Vishnu candi; (6) Garuda pavilion.

On a two-tiered base, bordered by 150 subsidiary
shrines, the three great cruciform vimanas are aligned
north–south with respect to each other to the west of the
centre of the site and facing their accompanying vahana
pavilions to the east. The Shiva candi has rooms in all four
projections, the eastern one forming a vestibule for the
central cella – as in earlier works like Candi Kalasan.
The patron's sepulchral chamber is below the centre of
the platform by the eastern steps to the Shiva candi.

There were 9th-century precedents for constructing a
vastupurusha accommodating the many gods of Meru in
separate cells, notably Candi Sewu where a single central
shrine was surrounded by 250 smaller ones on a square
terrace. Candi Sewu, however, was a Buddhist work not
unrelated to great terraced structures in and near the
Buddhist holy land, such as Paharpur in Bengal, or even
Nalanda – to which Indonesians are known to have gone
on pilgrimage.

part, in addition to candis, the Buddhists built stupas and monasteries. The early monastic buildings, usually of timber and brick, have disappeared and most of the stupas have been reduced to rubble. The great exception, and the crowning achievement of Javanese architecture, is the Mahayana mountain built c. 800 by an early Sailendra ruler at Borobodur.[79-83] The tripartite division of the candi is clear in the spendid relief progression through the tiered rectangles and tiered circles of its terraces to the stupa at the top, but the complex has no precise precedent other than in the mandala of the cosmos (see 6, page 19).

Nine pradakshina (circumambulatory) terraces, including the buried basement, transform a natural hill into the cosmic prasada, Meru, in accordance with a mandala determining the material and spiritual stages

78 **Parambanan, great temple complex** Shiva candi.
Much restored in the first campaign of extensive and still-continuing effort on the site, the main vimana of the great temple complex rises through a series of tiers. The sculpture is rich throughout the complex, the Ramayana panels of the main shrine being especially noteworthy.

79 **Borobodur, Great Stupa** c. 800, seen in the context of
the landscape.

80 **Borobodur, Great Stupa** aerial view.

81 **Borobodur, Great Stupa** square terrace.

82 **Borobodur, Great Stupa** circular terrace with latticed stupas and crowning stupa.

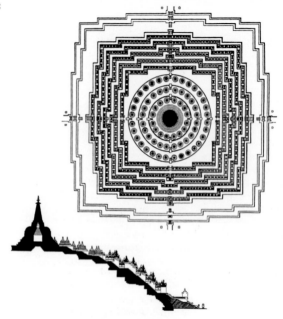

83 **Borobodur, Great Stupa** plan and section.

of the Buddhist quest for enlightenment. 150 metres (500 feet) long at base and diminishing as they ascend through a gentle curve in profile – like a stupa – the basement and first five galleried terraces are square, with shallow projections forming five bays on the lower three levels, three on the upper ones. They represent the material world. The last three are circular and open with 72 bell-shaped, latticed stupas in diminishing rings around the main stupa at the top. These are the zones of the spirit.

Magnificent reliefs in some 1300 panels, ranging from the realistic to the ethereal, embellish the retaining walls and outer galleries of the square levels, the buried one with images of earthly desire and its hellish consequences, the next five with scenes from the life of the Buddha – real and legendary – representing the stages of terrestrial existence. Images of the Buddha in the modes associated with guardianship of the directions of space are revealed in niches along the gallery parapets. The partial revelation of the Buddha's image through the lattice work of the stupas on the three circular, super-terrestrial zones presages the enlightenment achieved in extra-sensory apprehension of Buddhahood at the completely sealed crown-

ing stupa. The identity of the image found here –
indeed whether there was to be one at all – is the subject of considerable controversy. Seeing the mandala's
reduction of apparent multiplicity into the essential
oneness of the Buddha's supreme manifestation as
Vairocana, some have suggested that it was the apoth-
eosis of the Sailendra monarch, King of the Mountain,
as Devaraja, King of Meru – Universal Sovereign.

The early inhabitants of the peninsula known as Indo-China were animist too: they worshipped the spirits of ancestors, of trees, water, mountains, and later particularly of their sovereigns – 'Kings of the Mountain'. Indianisation came to them in at least three waves, and Buddhism and Hinduism alternated at the courts of Cambodia's kings throughout their several dynasties.

The influence of Ashoka's Buddhist missionaries spread south and east. From time immemorial Indian traders had established colonies on the Malay peninsula and around the Gulf of Thailand, as in the islands of Indonesia. In the 8th and 9th centuries AD, the power of Buddhist Srivijaya extended to Funan – the earliest Indo-Chinese kingdom – which straddled the Mekong delta of modern Cambodia, penetrated up-river towards modern Laos and reached westward through modern Thailand even to the Malay peninsula.

Funan

Funan is a Chinese name related phonetically to the native term for 'King of the Mountain'. According to Chinese sources, Funan was founded by an Indian called Kaundinya who married a local princess. He seems to have been styled Chandan, perhaps as relative to the Kushanas who bore that title. As we have seen, however, the natives worshipped the spirit of the mountain, and an ambitious ruler of foreign origin would naturally seek to identify himself with such a spirit, asserting his own divinity. To a Hindu pretender the mountain would, of course, be identified with cosmic Meru and it is this imagery that provides the key to understanding the imperial buildings of Funan's successors.

The kings of Funan followed the precedent of the Pallavas in surnaming themselves varman (protector). Their authority ran to instituting an integrated irrigation system, releasing large tracts of land from brackish flooding and seasonal desiccation. Their capital on the lower Mekong, Vyadhapura, was central to the first generation of the canals which were to play such an important part in the economic and architectural history of Cambodia.

The rise of Chenla

Before the assertion of Srivijanan ascendency, Funan ceded the middle Mekong to a rival power from the north which introduced the Khmers to the area's his-

tory. Known as Chenla to the Chinese, its first great
king, Isanavarman, founded his capital, Isanapura, at
modern Sambor in the area which was to remain the
centre of their power until beyond its apogee at
Angkor. Here, above all, they proved themselves great
water conservationists.

The names of the early Khmer kings of Chenla
betray the influence of the Pallavas. Unlike Funan's
Vyadapura, which seems to have been built of timber,
enough remains of Isanapura to trace the origins of
monumental architecture in the area, and here too
Pallavan influence is marked. As in Java, the principal
building type was the single cella prasada-vimana of
an Indian divinity and/or the deified ruler who was
buried below.

While the temples of Isanapura seem to recall the
brick buildings of the Buddhist holy land (the Mahabodhi at Bodh Gaya or its successors, such as the temple at Bhitargaon), the Shiva temple (also built of
brick) at Phnom Bayang[84] is clearly related to Mahaballipuram's late Pidari Ratha. A three-storey vimana
– like the Dharmaraja Ratha – it is built over an oblong
plan and consequently has a so-called keel roof, like
the Bhima Ratha (see 39, pages 108–09).

84 **Phnom Bayang, Shiva temple** 7th century, restored elevation.

The great age of the Khmers

Early in the 8th century Chenla absorbed Funan. Early in the 9th century its king, Jayavarman II, threw off the yoke of Srivijaya and, as Devaraja, initiated the great age of the Khmers. An incarnation of Shiva charged with maintaining the commonweal, he moved his seat to Phnom Kulen (just north of the Tonle Sap lake) under the symbol of Shiva's linga. Presaging later developments at Angkor, the town was a moated rectangle intersected by two main arteries oriented to the cardinal directions, with the main gate to the east and the main temple, enshrining the linga, next to the palace in the centre – as in the Kautilian ideal.

The ideal reasserted itself nearly a century later in the seats of Indravarman I (877–89) and his son Yashovarman I (889–900), each centred on a funerary temple reproducing the cosmic mountain as the repository of the Devaraja's sepulchre. These were the Bakong of Hariharalaya at Roluos,[85] south-east of Angkor, and the Bakheng of Yasodharapura at Angkor itself.[86] If the earliest monuments in the area had been ancestor shrines modelled on the primitive form of Hindu temple, the residence of the Purusha

85 **Angkor (Roluos), Bakong of Hariharalaya** c. 890,
view from the approach.

Indravarman I's first statement of the mountain theme
in the conception of the sepulchral temple consists of a
vimana derived from the early type of Funan, but cruciform
in plan and raised on a stepped pyramid of five terraces
ranging from 70 metres (230 feet) square at the base to
21 metres (69 feet) square to a height of 14 metres (47 feet).
The terraces originally carried miniature shrines echoing
the form of the main one.

This feature was further developed in the Bakheng
of Indravarman's son, in the centre of Yasodharapura,
where the main vimana was accompanied by four slightly
smaller ones on the corners of the top level and many more
miniature ones on the lower terraces. Obviously related
to the Great Stupa of Borobodur (see 80, page 205), the
conception as a whole was of a peak rising majestically
from foothills.

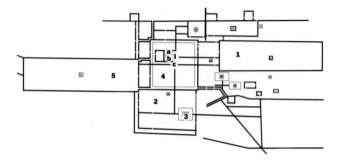

86 **Angkor** site plan.

(1) East Baray and Bakheng; (2) Yasodharapura,
with Bakheng; (3) Angkor Wat; (4) Angkor Thom with
(a) Phimeanakus; (b) Baphuon; (c) Bayon; (5) West Baray.

The 'cities', it should be noted, were precincts reserved
exclusively for cult and court ceremony. The people lived
beyond the walls and in the fields.

as prasada, the first imperial ones of the Khmer tradition honoured the divine spirit of the Mountain King in terms of the residence of the Purusha as cosmic Meru.

Moreover, Indravarman drained the Roluos into the artificial Lolei lake – some 3 kilometres long and 800 metres wide (1.8 miles by 2600 yards) – from which canals took water to Hariharalaya and the surrounding fields. His son began the even bigger East Baray (reservoir) to supply Yasodharapura at Angkor. Water management was achieved for the first time on an imperial scale by a divine king in virtue of the authority manifest in the mountain temple central to his seat.

Dissension ensued in the early 10th century, but Khmer imperial power was rehabilitated under Rajendravarman (944–68) and again under the usurper Suryavarman I (1002–50). The apogee was reached under Suryavarman II (1112–52). The cost of his wars, and his buildings, was enormous, and the reign ended in disaster, but decline was delayed until after the equally glorious, equally costly reign of Jayavarman VII (1180–1218).

Suryavarman I built or completed the Ta Keo moun-

87 **Angkor, Phimeanakus** probably completed in the early
12th century, view from the south.

tain temple and the palace platform known as Phimeanakus.[87] Its name meaning 'celestial palace', this stepped-pyramidal structure of three levels is too small to have been the Devaraja's mountain temple – and moreover is displaced from the town centre. Its single cruciform pavilion on the upper terrace was apparently built of timber and the edge of the top terrace was bordered by fenestrated galleries – also presumably of timber and derived from the vernacular trabeated tradition of small rooms linked by narrow corridors – which are unlikely to have been exclusively religious. This is the first time such galleries are known in monumental Khmer architecture, except for the Ta Keo where they border the lower terrace to frame the precinct for the five-towered temple mountain. The history of both these buildings is obscure, but they seem to have remained unfinished for several generations, at least until the reign of Suryavarman I.

If the Phimeanakus was a palace platform, it is the earliest surviving example of the Indian type, presumably of great antiquity, whose oldest distinguished representative in the subcontinent is the 16th-century Mahavamshi platform in the royal enclosure at Vijayanagar.

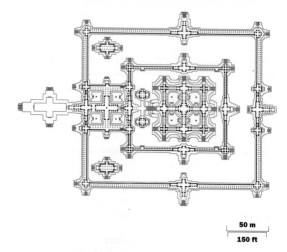

88 Angkor Wat plan.

Apart from myriad deities in niches and scenes from the great Indian epics on lintels and in tympana, apsaras and lotus foliage dance and ramp to unconstrained dominance in a repertory of motifs clearly related to the Indian water cosmology but nonetheless recalling native animism.

Angkor Thom and Angkor Wat

Doubtless Suryavarman had a new capital in mind, but this was not realised until the reign of his son, Udaya-dityavarman II (1050–66). Partly replacing Yasod-harapura on a reduced scale, and known as Angkor Thom, this was centred around the Baphuon mountain temple, built beside the Phimeanakus, and its inhabitants were served by the largest of all Khmer tanks, Angkor's West Baray.

Suryavarman II rehabilitated Angkor Thom, the most substantial surviving representative of the ancient Indian ideal town, preserving the Phimeanakus in its centre. And to the south, in the south-east quarter of old Yasodharapura, he made the supreme statement of the Mountain King's cosmic ideal in Hindu terms, Angkor Wat.

The main spaces of this stupendous structure are external – courts and cloistered precincts.[88–90] The internal spaces – the garbha-grihas – are restricted by the degree they can be corbelled in sandstone, and by a supreme exclusiveness. Columns are simple square

89 OVERLEAF **Angkor Wat** view from the west over the moat to the main entrance.

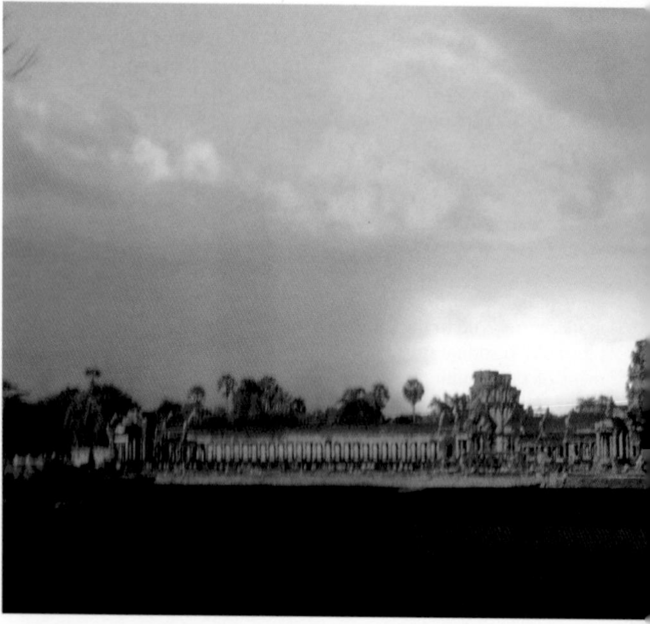

90 **Angkor Wat** aerial view.

SURYAVARMAN II's mature statement of the sepulchral mountain temple is contained in a compound 4 kilometres (2½ miles) in circumference. The causeway over the moat from the west, with its balustrade of demons holding extended nagas, leads to a great cruciform portico. Beyond, a colonnaded gallery of the kind first encountered at the Ta Keo, but facing outwards and some 800 metres (2600 feet) in extent, frames the precinct with a frieze of dynastic narrative mainly related in terms of the Ramayana and Mahabharata epics. Within a second cruciform gate in the centre of the cloister's west range, at a higher level, are a pair of pavilions and a square court divided by galleries. This is the prelude to the main precinct, which is defined by another cloistered gallery with vimanas at the corners. East of the precinct's centre, beyond a pair of chapels, the precipitous pyramid of the main mountain temple is crowned by five nine-tiered vimanas united by another, grander grid of galleries. The central peak soars some 61 metres (200 feet) at the culmination of a progression of vimanas, similar in stellate plan and parabolic profile but graded in scale to enhance its impact. It enshrined the Devaraja as Vishnu – in whose entourage Surya is chief luminary – above a profound shaft representing the axis of the world.

91 **Angkor Wat** details of embellishment.

posts carrying a corbel bracket to spread the load, but windows are screened by elegantly turned slats. Gabled roofs, usually with a makara profile, are telescoped at the transition from one plane to another – indeed, the superimposition of multiple gables at a reduced scale was a major motif. Internal walls are plain, external surfaces are chiselled with exceptionally fine reliefs.[91] Never have colossal scale and intimacy of detail been so convincingly combined.

The last word was left to the Buddhist Jayavarman VII. He remodelled Angkor Thom,[92] destroyed by foreign invaders after the death of Suryavarman II, and gave it a new centre: the extraordinary anthropomorphic Bayon[93] which, like the gates to the town itself,[94] asserted the king's identity with the bodhisattva Avalokiteshvara. The final statement of the Khmer sepulchral mountain temple was built in three stages. Only the outer cloister remains of the first campaign. Sixteen chapels, now largely gone, were then built to connect this to a raised central precinct (again, only parts of the enclosing cloister, which seems to have been square with cruciform projections, survive). To mark the triumph of Buddhism and the restoration of Angkor, finally, Jayavarman built the sanctuary, with

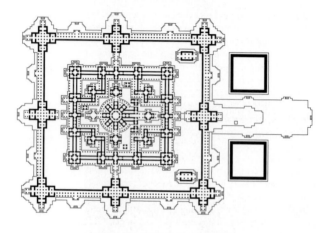

92 **Angkor Thom, Bayon** c. 1200, plan.

93 **Angkor Thom, Bayon** central tower.

its circular base, radiating cruciform chapels and vestibule. The Devaraja was, of course, enshrined at the centre and the chapels were dedicated to the imperial provinces: above superb reliefs, all were crowned with four-faced towers representing the king as Buddha Lokesvara (lord of the world). The radiation of divine power to all points of the compass is inescapable.

The country had embraced Buddhism again, but after Jayarvarman it turned from the god-king towards a primitive simplicity, essentially anti-monumental.

94 **Angkor Thom** gate.

In his reconstruction of the moated town, centred on the Bayon, Jayavarman expressed it as the precinct of sanctuary in impressing the face of divine rule on the gates which open the main axes at the cardinal points in its square perimeter. A fifth gate, in the east range, opened the route to the Phimeanakus. The peaked gates have been interpreted as representing the subsidiary range surrounding Meru, the *axis mundi* itself represented by the Bayon of course, and the moat as the primordial ocean – the Sea of Milk whose churning by the axial pestle, generating life, may be seen as re-enacted by the demons hauling on rope-like nagas along the causeways.

By the time of Ashoka – the mid 3rd century BC – two different waves of people had moved into the lands now constituting Myanmar (Burma). Easterners related to the Khmer and known as Mons had passed through central Thailand and founded a kingdom around the port of Thaton, at the head of the Andaman Sea, east of the great Irrawaddi delta. Northerners of Tibetan origin had overcome the native Burmese and formed several states in Upper Burma. Led by a tribe known as Pyu, they went on to establish a kingdom – rather a confederation of principalities – centred on Sri Ksetra near Prome, at the apex of the

95 **Bagan, Ananda Pahto** view of the interior from the porch through the ambulatory to the sanctuary.

Four colossal standing images of the Buddha face the cardinal directions from the cellas through the porches which extend the basic square to a Greek cross.

Virtually unknown in ancient India, with the most notable exceptions of Bodh Gaya and Bhirargoan, arches are not uncharacteristic of the architecture of ancient Myanmar. Nevertheless, an Indian precedent for the form here may be detected in the great cruciform terraced brick temple at Paharpur in Bengal.

Irrawaddi delta, by the end of the millennium. Controlling the Irrawaddi, they held the key to the trade route which linked China to India through northern Burma. Indian ideas came that way and, ultimately, by sea and through the ports of the great river. Likewise, it was through Thaton that the Mons forged their links with the Buddhist realm of the Mauryas. They found that the way of the Buddha, originally traced with the guidance of nature spirits native to the Ganges basin, could readily accommodate their own animism and they accepted the Indian model for kingship.

Invasion and conversion

Nearly a thousand years of mainly peaceful intercourse with India saw the introduction of Hinduism as well as Mahayana Buddhism. By the middle of the first millennium AD, the essentially tribal Pyus had extended their confederation to the Mons but before the end of the 6th century the silting of the delta led to rivalry for the island of Pegu, which had emerged at the new mouth of the river. More solidly monarchical, the Mons won and went on to dominate the whole of southern Burma from Pegu. The Pyu, forced from their land-locked capital, retreated to Upper Burma and succumbed to invaders from southern China early in the 9th century. The native Burmese reasserted themselves and founded the capital of their own kingdom at Bagan in 849.

Meanwhile the Theravada Buddhist tradition of Ashoka's age had long been eclipsed by the Mahayana in India and the Mahayana in turn was being eclipsed by Hinduism. The primitive orthodoxy was sustained in Sri Lanka, and with it the tradition of the unembellished stupa.[96] However, though certainly not unchallenged by Hinduism, the Mahayana stretched through the land of the Pyus to the rest of south-east Asia except for the kingdom of the Mons which maintained close relations with Sri Lanka. His faith under duress, a monk from Pegu, who had trained in Sri Lanka, went on the offensive to Bagan and converted the new king, Anawrahta (1044–77). Anawrahta took the Burmese back to the old faith, went on to conquer his Mahayana neighbours, absorbed the Mons and unified the country now known as Myanmar for the first time.

The empire of Bagan was overwhelmed by the Mongols from China at the end of the 13th century. Unity was restored, though partially and briefly, in the 16th

96 **Anuradhapura, Thuparama dagoba** elevation.

Although Sri Lanka was richly endowed by its princes
for more than 2000 years, its architectural heritage is
dominated by little more impressive than the remains of
the great stupas at its ancient capitals, Anuradhapura
(from the 3rd century BC until the 8th century AD) and
Polonnaruwa (from the 8th to the 15th century). Generally
bell-shaped, the typical Sinhalese stupa (dagoba) has three
main zones: the splayed base, itself divided into three
terraces below a ringed medhi; the domical anda, often
with a pronounced bulge; the square harmika with its
protective chattravali, the seven-tiered umbrellas of which
are stylised into a ringed cone and surmounted with a bud-
shaped element. The Thuparama at Anuradhapura well
represents the form. It was reputedly founded in 244 BC,
shortly after Buddhism was introduced to the island by
Ashoka's son, Mahinda, but has subsequently been much
augmented like the Mauryan stupas of India. The great
stupas of the Andhras at Amaravati and Nagajunakonda,
where Sinhalese monks regularly went for training, were
the dominant influence when Anuradhapura was at its
height though the Mahayana embellishment there was
foreign to the Hinayana tradition which remained
predominant in Sri Lanka.

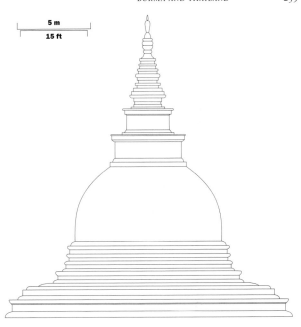

5 m

15 ft

century under Dayinnaung of Pegu, more-enduringly
by Alaungpaya, who established Rangoon in the mid
18th century, and then under the British in the 19th
century. Buddhism persisted throughout but the
resources of the divided land usually ran only to
ephemeral constructions in wood for monastery and
palace. Unity, however, was commemorated in brick,
plaster and gold nowhere more prolifically than at
Bagan, nowhere more brilliantly than at Rangoon.

97 OVERLEAF **Bagan** view from Mimalaung Kyaung at
the centre of the walled city with Thatbyinnyu Pahto
(centre), Ananda Pahto (left background), Nathlaung
Kyaung (right), and Thamya Pahto (right foreground),
beyond various zedis.

Built over an older Pyu site, Burmese Bagan seems to
have been walled from its foundation towards the middle
of the 9th century. Among the oldest surviving temples in
the walled area, the Nathlaung Kyaung is the only one
dedicated to Vishnu, indeed it is the only Hindu pahto
in the vicinity. Built c. 931, its ambulatory-enclosed cella
is four-faced like works at the Pyu capital, Sri Ksetra.
Still following the Pyu formula, but with a bulbous stupa
instead of a sikhara, the Thamya Pahto is attributed to

Bagan

More than 4000 shrines have been counted at Bagan.[97] There are two basic types: stupas (zedis) and temples (pahtos). The pahtos may have one entrance and vestibule to a single cella or four entrances and four cellas linked by an enclosed ambulatory path and in the grandest works the ambulatory surrounds a central cella or cella complex on several levels.[98] The earliest ones follow largely lost Pyu precedents, them-

Anawrahta's able follower Kyanzittha (1084–1113).

Kyanzittha's even more-impressive successor, Anawrahta's great-grandson Alaungsithu (1113–67), contributed the Thatbyinnyu Pahto, one of the largest at the site. Prasada-like, it has four Buddha images in cellas on two main levels, with ambulatories surmounted by galleries, and both main blocks have terraces bordered with miniature shrines; the stupa tower rises to 61 metres (200 feet). The temple at Paharpur is a likely precedent for this Burmese permutation of the Indian multi-storey prasada but it may well also have been influenced by the Mons whose limited architectural legacy includes multi-storeyed stepped-pyramidal reliquary shrines – such as the one at Vat Ku Kut at Lamphun in Thailand.

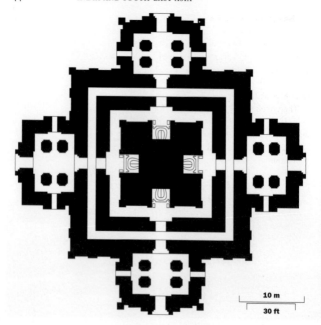

98 **Bagan, Ananda Pahto** c. 1100, plan and view
of the main prasada from the south-west (OVERLEAF).

Built towards the middle of Kyanzittha's reign, the
cubical mass – 53 metres (174 feet) each side – has a solid
brick core, four cellas and double ambulatories with arched
vaults. Porches facing the cardinal points extend the basic
square to a Greek cross.

The massive walls enclosing the ambulatories are graded
in height, their gently curved profiles stepping up to the
platform over the main central block. A Latina-type sikhara,
gilded in 1990 to commemorate the 900th anniversary of
the temple's foundation, rises to 51 metres (167 feet) over
a stepped pyramidal base. It is reproduced to a smaller scale
on the four corners of the upper terrace but still-smaller
stupas mark the corners of the lower zones. The brickwork
is reinforced with stone, especially for the voussoires of the
arched vaults in the porches and ambulatories.

selves endebted to the primitive Indian arca-griha. Surmounted by a sikhara or a stupa, the more sophisti-
cated later ones descend from the Indian prasada,
perhaps via the Mons who seem to have favoured
stepped pyramids for their reliquary shrines. The
descent is usually remote – and the detail often coarse
– but at the very centre of the walled city is a facsim-
ile of the Mahabodhi prototype.[99]

The stupas occasionally recall lost subcontinental
Mahayana masterpieces like those of Nagarjunakon-
da or Amaravati[100] but they more usually acknowl-
edge the influence of orthodox Sri Lanka in their
bell-shaped, sometimes bulbous, form.[101] This may

99 **Bagan, Mahabodhi Paya** c. 1220.

Built towards the end of the Bagan empire by
Nantaungmya (1211–34), this is one of several
contemporary Burmese copies of the Mahabodhi Temple
at Gaya, for the restoration of which the Burmese assumed
responsibility at various reprises after the decline of
Buddhism in India. It seems unlikely that they contributed
the arches which reinforce the original Mahabodhi's
structure, uncharacteristically for India, but they could well
have determined the form of the crowning stupa there.

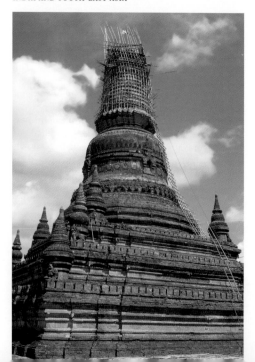

well have come with reliquary caskets but there was a steady flow of monks between Hinayana centres.

The characteristically Burmese permutation of the stupa, with the elegantly splayed base even more elaborately tiered than the Sinhalese norm, has a richly incised anda over multiple ring-like medhis and an extremely attenuated chattravali rising from further dimininishing rings. Its evolution may be traced at Bagan but reaches its apogee in Rangoon where the gilded Shwe Dagon outshines all else.[102]

By the middle of the first millennium ad, commercial contacts between India, Sri Lanka and the land now constituting Thailand led to the introduction of both Buddhism and Hinduism – and the buildings which served them. From the 5th to the 8th centuries

100 **Bagan, Seinnyet Nyima Paya** 13th century?
view from the south-west.

Clearly recalling the great Indian Andhran tradition of works like the Mahastupa of Amaravati in the embellishment of its anda, this work is attributed to the 11th-century Queen Seinnyet but appears to have been rebuilt later – or, like the great Amaravati work, transformed by new embellishment.

101 **Bagan, Shwezigon Paya** second half of the
11th century.

Commissioned by Anawrahta in 1059 as a reliquary
for a copy of the Buddha's tooth enshrined in Kandy
(Sri Lanka), this stupa was completed well into the reign
of Kyanzittha. On three superimposed terraces, the anda's
base is embellished with Jataka episodes in glazed terracotta
panels, and four bronze images of the standing Buddha
(4 metres – 13 feet – high) which face the four staircases in
the cardinal directions. Like the Shwesandaw Paya (built
from 1057 outside the walls of Bagan to commemorate
Anawrahta's conquest of the Mon capital Thaton) and most
of the other stupas at the site, the bell-shaped anda recalls
the typical Sinhalese form. The transition from rectangle
to circle recalls Borobodor but there is an intermediate
octagonal zone. The elaboration of the base, the four
staircases at the cardinal points and the superimposition
of multiple rings over the anda, perhaps in memory of the
chattravali, mark the start of the evolution of the specifically
Burmese zedi.

With a more broadly based anda, the Shwezigon Paya
is weightier in its monumentality than the elegant
Shwesandaw Paya but the future lay with the latter.

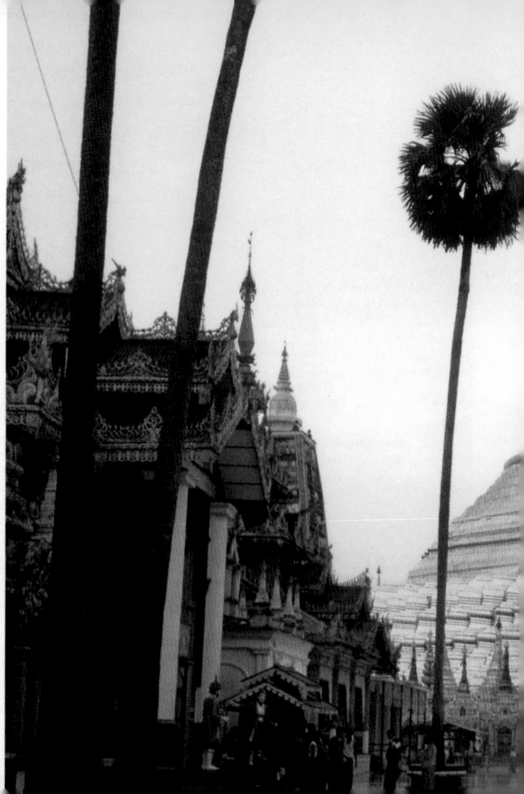

102 PREVIOUS PAGES **Rangoon, Shwe Dagon pagoda.**

Originally built by the Mons some time in the second
half of the first millennium AD to enshrine miraculously
rediscovered hairs of the Buddha, Rangoon's major
monument dates in its present form from 1769 (though
repaired and regilded many times since). An inscription
of 1485 records a visit of Anawrahta of Bagan in the
second half of the 11th century, major reconstruction
under the southern king Bayinnaung in the second half of
the 14th century, in which it reached a height of 18 metres
(59 feet), and various 15th-century campaigns which took
it to 90m, nearly its present height. Earthquakes prompted
most of the rebuilding campaigns. It seems first to have
been gilded in the 15th century and is now estimated to
be sheathed in more than 50 metric tons of gold.

Towards the southern side of its rectangular platform,
surrounded by hundreds of other stupas and shrines, the
6.5-metre- (21-foot-) high plinth is bordered with 60 small
stupas and four larger ones marking the cardinal directions.
Square with recessed corners, the plinth supports multiple
octagonal terraces, contracted medhi rings, the bell-shaped
anda, a cone of further superimposed rings, lotus petals
turned both up and down, a bud-shaped member and the
stylised seven-tiered umbrella (hti) studded with diamonds.

much of the area was under the control of the Mons whose stepped pyramidal form of reliquary prasadas may well lie behind structures like the Thatbyinnyu Pahto. Little remains from this period or the following three centuries of Sri Vijayan dominance. The three centruies after that were predominantly Khmer, politically and culturally.

Thailand

Meanwhile the Thai people from southern China had been penetrating the peninsula and mingling with the Mons. With the Khmers in disarray, they established several small states of which Lan Na in the north and Sukhothai further south, towards the centre of the present kingdom, had emerged predominant by the 14th century. Both followed Khmer precedents in temple and town planning but the Mon stepped-pyramidal tradition was sustained in Lan Na. As the Sukhothai were Theravadin Buddhists they maintained close relations with Sri Lanka. Thus their sacred precincts were dominated by bell-shaped stupas, as an alternative to cone or cob-shaped towers, and the Sukhothai are generally credited with developing from this dual inheritance the forms which were to be characteristi-

103 Typical Thai reliquary shrines.

(1) Mon reliquary shrine. Chedi Suwan Chang Kot (traditionally dated to 755, restored in 1218) in the Wat Ku Kut (Wat Cham Thewi) at Lamphun is an outstanding example.

(2) Sukhothai chedi. The chedi of Wat Chang Lom near Sawankalok (dated variously to the end of the 13th century and up to 200 years later) well represents the classic Sukhothai type. If the earlier date is correct, this is the earliest-known example of the Sinhalese bell-shaped type in Thailand.

(3) Ayutthaya chedi. Two late 15th-century examples

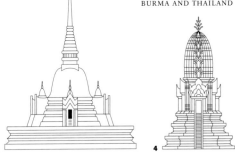

3   4

and one from the mid 16th century are to be found side-by-side in the Wat Phra Si Sanphet at Ayutthaya.

(4) Prang. An early, somewhat squat, example of the Khmer type is to be found in the Wat Sri Sawai at Sukhothai (dated variously from the 12th to the 14th century but more probably the latter). The prototype for Thai development of the form is generally identified as the early 15th-century example in Wat Ratchaburana at Ayutthaya. A later example (extensively restored in the 18th century), with high tiered base and seven-storeyed sikhara, is to be found in the Wat Phra Sri Ratana Mahathat near Sawankhalok.

cally Thai.[103] As they built of wood or brick and stucco, little of their architecture survives.

In 1351 a new Thai dynasty moved the capital south to Ayutthaya, nearer the sea – trade and confidence both having grown. Politically and culturally the achievements of the Sukhothai were consolidated and extended. Ayutthaya was destroyed by the Burmese under King Alaungpaya in 1767. Rama I, founder of the Chakri dynasty in 1782, built his new capital in conscious emulation of Ayutthaya at nearby Bangkok.

Thai monuments

The rulers of Ayutthaya and their successors were responsible for the country's most substantial remaining monuments. In and beyond the capitals, the major centres of activity were monasteries (wats). In a walled compound, a number of halls (mondop=mandapa) are invariably dominated by a reliquary building, which may be a stupa (chedi) or a tower (prang). The former are most usually bell-shaped on terraced platforms with square harmika and ringed, conical chattravali , as in Burma after the Sinhalese fashion probably imported with reliquary caskets (see 103, page 258–59). Under the Sukhothai, however, the relic was sometimes moved from the harmika to a faceted medhi on a tiered plinth as well as a terraced base and the anda took on the lotus bud form, tapering directly into the chattravali. This assimilated it to the other alternative reliquary building, the prang: a tower of the Khmer cob-shaped form (prasad=prasada), usually of six storeys and a niched cella on tiered and faceted socle and plinth, which ultimately derived from the Indian sikhara.

In the Khmer manner too, the typical hall of the Thai wat is an elongated trabeated structure with multiple tiered roofs, often walled for protection rather than solidity. The principal one is the ordination hall (ubosot) with eight lotiform stones or colonnettes (bai sema) demarkating the consecrated ground. Others are for assembly (wihan=vihara, but the type is not generally residential in Thailand). For the library or a special relic there is also usually a square pavilion with a pyramid of tiered roofs terminating in a spire. All shelter images of the Buddha as if enthroned in an audience hall. The grandest ordination hall dominates the most splendid of all Thai temples, the Wat Phra Kaeo in Bangkok.[104-105] The throne room of the royal palace is of the same type, as it is in Cambodia.

104 **Bangkok, royal palace precinct of the Temple
of the Emerald Buddha.**

Multiplied to a standard formula in the Ayutthaya period, the traditional forms were retained for the new capital but as wealth increased and the 19th century unfolded, prolixity increased. Simple circular forms gave way to elaborate faceting, plain plastered or gilt surfaces to rich carving and polychrome tilework. Roof was superimposed on roof, as in a pagoda but over plans of all shapes, and when they were gabled they were fringed with intricate bargeboards stamped

105 OVERLEAF **Bangkok, Grand Palace compound, Wat Phra Kaeo.**

The ubosot (right) of the royal palatine temple was built by Rama I (1782–1809) to house the Emerald Buddha (Phra Kaeo Morokot, a jade statuette first recorded in 1434). The Phra Sri Ratna Chedi of 1855 (centre foreground), was modelled on the classic Ayutthaya examples of the Wat Phra Sri Sanphet. Prasat Phra Thep Bidon, the cruciform building crowned with a prang (left background) was built by Rama IV (Mongkut, 1851–68) and converted into a pantheon for statues of the Chakri dynasty by Rama V (Chulalongkorn, 1868–1910). Between the chedi and the prang rises the spire of the Phra Mondop library built by Rama III (1824–51).

106 **Djogdjakarta, royal palace (kraton)** interior of 19th-century audience hall.

with the iconography of the ancient water-cosmology inherited by Buddhism with the yakshas and nagas so sagely wooed by Siddhartha Gautama.

The oldest of imported Indian monumental forms, the stupa, rises predominant from the plethora in Thailand and Cambodia, as in Burma. Even older is the mandapa which shelters the image of the deity as it always sheltered the Indian king. And those who would take him for their model are widespread indeed.[106]

glossary

ABACUS flat slab forming the top of a CAPITAL.

ACROPOLIS highest part or CITADEL of a city, usually the area containing the principal public buildings.

AEDICULE ornamental pilastered niche to house a sacred image for example.

AISLE side passage of a temple, running parallel to the NAVE and separated from it by COLUMNS or PIERS.

AMBULATORY semi-circular or polygonal arcade or walkway.

ANDA burial mound at the centre of a STUPA, usually in the form of a solid dome.

ANTARALA passage or vestibule before a sanctuary in a Hindu temple.

APADANA columned HYPOSTYLE HALL, usually square in plan, with a PORTICO to one or more sides.

APSE semi-circular domed or vaulted space, especially at one end of a BASILICA. Hence APSIDAL, in the shape of an APSE.

ARCA-GRIHA image-chamber in a Buddhist shrine.

ARCADE series of arches supported by COLUMNS, sometimes paired and covered so as to form a walkway.

ARCHITRAVE one of the three principal elements of an ENTABLATURE, positioned immediately above the CAPITAL of a COLUMN, and supporting the FRIEZE and CORNICE.

ARCUATE shaped like an arch. Hence (of a building) arcuated, deploying arch structures (as opposed to TRABEATED).

ASTRAGAL small MOULDING with circular or semi-circular cross-section.

AVARANA-DEVATA attendant or subsidiary deity in the Hindu pantheon.

AXIS MUNDI pole of the god Indra in Vedic iconography.

AYODHYA generic Vedic term for city of the gods.

BARBICAN fortified structure at the entry to a town or city, often straddling a gateway.

BARGEBOARD board – usually decorated – sited at the gable end of the pitches of a roof.

BASILICA temple or other public building, consisting principally of a COLONNADED rectangular space enclosed by an AMBULATORY or having a central NAVE and side AISLES, often with an APSE and generally lit by a CLERESTORY.

BASTION structure projecting from the angle of a defensive wall, enabling enhanced vision and mobility for a garrison.

BATTERING reinforcement of wall bases by building a sloping supporting structure.

BEAM horizontal element in, for instance, a TRABEATED structure.

BHUMIJA type of northern Hindu temple superstructure composed of superimposed rows of miniature shrine motifs between vertical bands. (See page 121.)

BODHISATTVA previous incarnation of the Buddha, a compassionate spirit.

CANDI Indo-Indonesian royal sepulchre.

CAPITAL top part of a COLUMN, supporting the ENTABLATURE.

CELLA the sanctuary of a temple, usually containing the cult statue.

CHADYA awning, eave.

CHAITYA shrine or other sacred place or object.

CHAITYA-GRIHA type of Buddhist shrine evolved from a meeting-hall.

CHANKAMA/CHANKYAMA promenade.

CHATRAVALI tiers forming the CHATTRI on top of the mound of a STUPA.

CHATTRI an umbrella-shaped dome or pavilion, sometimes acting as a turret on the roof of a STUPA.

CHATURMUKHA four-sided temple.

CITADEL fortress, usually at the highest part of a town.

CLERESTORY windowed upper level, providing light for a double-storey interior.

CLOISTER covered ARCADE, often running around the perimeter of an open courtyard.

COLONNADE line of regularly spaced COLUMNS.

COLUMN vertical member, usually circular in cross-section, functionally structural or ornamental or both, comprising a base, shaft and CAPITAL.

CORBEL course of masonry or support bracket, usually stone, for BEAM or other horizontal member. Hence corbelled, forming a stepped roof by deploying progressively overlapping CORBELS.

CORNICE projecting moulding forming the top part of an ENTABLATURE.

CRENELLATION indentation in the upper part of a battlement.

CREPIDOMA steps forming the platform of a temple.

CUPOLA hemispherical dome forming the roof of all or (especially a relatively small) part of a building which may not itself be of circular plan.

CUSP projection formed between two arcs, especially in stone tracery, hence CUSPED.

CYMA RECTA wave-shaped moulding, usually forming all or part of a CORNICE, the upper part convex and the lower concave.

CYMA REVERSA wave-shaped moulding, usually forming all or part of a CORNICE, the upper part concave and the lower convex.

DADO the middle part, between base and CORNICE, of a PEDESTAL or the lower part of a wall when treated as a continuous pedestal.

DHARMA law, doctrine, or righteousness.

DISTYLE a PORTICO with two COLUMNS.

DORMER rectilinear horizontal/vertical structure piercing a sloping roof.

DURBAR royal assembly or audience.

DVARA door.

EAVES the part of a roof which overhangs the outer face of a wall.

EMBRASURE an opening or indentation in a wall or PARAPET.

ENTABLATURE part of the façade immediately above the COLUMNS, usually composed of a supportive ARCHITRAVE, decorative FRIEZE and projecting CORNICE.

FILIGREE decorative work formed from a mesh or by piercing material to give the impression of a mesh.

FINIAL ornament at the top of a gable or roof, for example.

FRIEZE the middle part of an ENTABLATURE, above the ARCHITRAVE and below the CORNICE, or more generally any horizontal strip decorated in RELIEF.

GARBHA-GRIHA small square space serving as the inner sanctum of a Hindu temple.

GAVAKSHA LUNETTE or horseshoe-shaped window or gable.

GHANADVARA false or blind door in Hindu temple. (See page 104.)

GOPURA gate-house to temple.

HAMSA goose in Vedic iconography.

HAREM women's quarters.

HARMIKA part of the structure of a STUPA.

HINAYANA the lesser vehicle towards salvation in the Buddhist tradition (as opposed to MAHAYANA). (See pages 54, 55.)

HYPOSTYLE HALL hall with a roof supported by numerous COLUMNS more or less evenly spaced across its area.

IWAN vaulted hall or recess opening off a court.

JALI lattice or FILIGREE-patterned screen.

KALASHA water pitcher or vase in Vedic iconography.

KAPOTA EAVE-like cornice.

KARNAKA pointed ASTRAGAL MOULDING.

KHURA floor slab with curved shoulder. (See pages 94, 95.)

KIRTIMUKHA/KIRTTIMUKHA leonine monster in Vedic cosmology, and hence stylised representation thereof.

KRATON court of early Indonesian rulers.

KUMBHA bulbous water pot, and hence derivative TORUS MOULDING.

KUMUDA TORUS MOULDING either semi-circular or chamfered (alternative term for KUMBHA, especially in the south).

KUTAGARA pavilion on the terrace of a palace.

LATA creeper, and hence a particular style of decorative band in the Hindu temple architectural tradition. (See page 121.)

LATINA/LATINA type of northern Hindu temple superstructure composed of a single body (as opposed to SEKHARI or BHUNIJA). (See page 121.)

LEOGRYPH fabulous creature with the physical characteristics of a lion.

LINGA phallic emblem, most frequently occurring symbol of Shiva in Hindu iconography.

LINTEL horizontal member over for example a window or doorway or bridging the gap between two COLUMNS or PIERS.

LUNETTE semi-circular window or recess, usually at the base of a dome or vault.

MACHICOLATION gallery or PARAPET projecting on CORBELS from the outside of defensive walls, with holes for missiles to be dropped or thrown.

MAHAL summer-house or pavilion.

MAHAYANA the great vehicle towards salvation in the Buddhist tradition (as opposed to HINAYANA). (See pages 54, 55.)

MAIDAN open field before fort or palace, hence civic park.

MAKARA crocodile-like monster in Vedic iconography.

MAKARA-TORANA doorway embellished with MAKARA carvings.

MANDALA magical diagram.

MANDAPA hall or pillared pavilion.

MEDHI drum forming the base of a STUPA. (See page 35.)

MERLONS raised elements of a battlement, alternating with EMBRASURES.

MITHUNA representation of intimate couple – sometimes shown engaged in sexual intercourse.

MOKSHA liberation or release.

MOULDING the contour of a projecting or inset element.

MULAPRASADA main block of a temple, containing a shrine.

NAGA fabulous serpent in Vedic iconography.

NAGA-TORANA doorway embellished with NAGA carvings.

NAVE central body of principal interior of, for instance, a temple.

NIRVANA in the Buddhist tradition, the blissful end to the human struggle.

ORDER defining feature of architecture, comprising a COLUMN together with its ENTABLATURE.

PADMA lotus, hence also derived CYMA RECTA or CYMA REVERSA MOULDING.

PADMA-KUMBHA combination of MOULDINGS characteristic of for example CAPITALS in Hindu temples.

PADMALATA bowl with trailing lotus vines in Vedic iconography.

PANCHAYATANA five-shrine temple complex in the Hindu tradition.

PARAPET low wall, usually for defensive purposes.

PARSHVA-DEVATA/PARSHVA DEVATA aspects of the deity in Hindu iconography.

PEDESTAL base supporting, for example, a COLUMN or statue.

PEDIMENT: triangular area of wall above the ENTABLATURE.

PHAMSANA stepped pyramidal type of roof with rectilinear profile.

PIER supporting pillar for wall or roof, often of rectangular cross-section.

PILASTER a PIER of rectangular cross-section, more or less integral with and only slightly projecting from the wall which it supports.

PLINTH rectangular base or base support of a COLUMN or wall.

PODIUM continuous base or PEDESTAL consisting of PLINTH, DADO and CORNICE, to support a series of COLUMNS.

PORTAL doorway, usually on the grand scale.

PORTICO entrance to a building featuring a COLONNADE

POST vertical element in for instance a TRABEATED structure.

PRADAKSHINA AMBULATORY in Buddhist monastery.

PRADAKSHINA-PATHA circumambulatory path or passage around a shrine.

PRAGGRIVA porch of a Hindu temple.

PRASADA multi-storey structure: mansion, palace or temple.

PRASADA-VIMANA palace in a sacred environment, as in a tomb building for example.

PUJA worship.

PURNA-KALASHA bowl of plenty in Vedic iconography.

RAKING CORNICE an inclined CORNICE, deployed above the TYMPANUM of a PEDIMENT.

RATHA ritual chariot in Hindu temple.

RATHIKA niche or AEDICULE.

RELIEF carving, typically of figures, raised from a flat background usually by cutting away more (high relief) or less (low relief) of the material from which they are carved.

REVETMENT decorative reinforced facing for retaining wall.

SAMVARANA pyramidal hall roof with tiers of bell-shaped mouldings.

SANGHA order of monks, especially Buddhist, hence SANGHARAMA abode of Buddhist order, monastery.

SARDULA leogryph in Hindu iconography.

SEKHARI type of northern Hindu temple superstructure composed of a cluster of spire-like forms (as opposed to LATINA). (See page 121.)

SERDAB subterranean room.

SHAKHA conceptualised branches depicted in the principal members of a temple doorway in Vedic iconography. (See pages 11, 12.)

SHAKTI active or imminent aspect of deity personified as consort in Hindu iconography.

SHASTRA architectural treatise in Vedic literature.

SHIKHARA superstructure of a Northern Hindu temple.

SOCLE base or PEDESTAL.

STAMBHA pillar or post.

STRING COURSE projecting horizontal course of structural elements or MOULDING.

STUPA pre-eminent type of Buddhist monument, a TUMULUS, burial or reliquary mound, always freestanding, characteristically comprising a circular drum (MEDHI) forming the base for a massive solid dome (ANDA), topped by a turret (CHATTRI).

STYLOBATE top step of a CREPIDOMA, forming the base for a COLONNADE.

SWASTIKA cross in fragmentary squares, symbol of solar movement.

TANTRISM Buddhist doctrine associated with a group of mystical works – the tantras.

TIRTHA in the Hindu tradition a fording place, place of spiritual regeneration, and hence a temple, thus TIRTHANKARA ford-maker.

TORANA ceremonial portal or portal motif.

TORUS large convex moulding, typically at the base of a COLUMN, of more or less semi-circular cross-section.

TRABEATED structurally dependent on rectilinear POST and BEAM supports.

TRANSOM cross-bar or LINTEL, especially of a window.

TUMULUS ancient burial mound.

TYMPANUM triangular area of a PEDIMENT enclosed by CORNICES above and ENTABLATURE below; an area, usually recessed, formed by a LINTEL below and an arch above.

VAHANA vehicle or mount of a god.

VAJRA thunderbolt of the god Indra in the Vedic tradition.

VASTU residence.

VASTUPURUSHA residence of the gods, especially as embodied in Vedic literature.

VASTUPURUSHAMANDALA diagram for the residence of the purusha, the formula for sacred building.

VASTUSHASTRA traditional science of architecture.

VAULT structure forming an arched roof over a space.

VEDIKA railing, especially of sacred enclosure.

VERANDAH roofed COLONNADE attached to one or more sides of a building.

VIHARA residential quarters of Buddhist monastery.

VIMANA storeyed building with receding terraces, used in the south as main element of sanctuary (equivalent to northern MULAPRASADA).

VOLUTE scroll or spiral ornamental and/or support member.

VYALA lion or leopard in Hindu iconography.

WAT Buddhist temple/monastery, particularly in Thailand.

WATTLE AND DAUB method of making walls using thin twigs (wattles) interwoven and then plastered with mud or clay (daub).

YAKSHA masculine tree spirit.

YAKSHINI feminine tree spirit.

YASHTI shaft or mast associated with the god Indra.

YOGINI embodiments of working energy in Hindu iconography, subservient to SHAKTI.

ZENANA enclosed accommodation for women.

The books listed below are those the author found particularly useful as sources of general information on the architecture covered in this volume.

Brown, P, *Indian Architecture*, volume 1: Buddhist and Hindu, Bombay 1942 and subsequent editions

Coomaraswamy, A K, *Early Indian Architecture: Palaces*, Delhi 1975

Deva, K, *Temples of North India*, Delhi 1969

Dhaky, M A and Meister, M, eds, *Encyclopaedia of Hindu Temple Architecture*, Delhi 1983

Frédéric, Louis, *The Temples and Sculpture of Southeast Asia*, London 1965

Harle, J C, *The Art and Architecture of the Indian Subcontinent*, Harmondsworth 1986

Huntington, S L and J C, *The Art of Ancient India*, New York 1985

Kramrisch, S, *The Hindu Temple*, London 1954

Mitchell, D, *The Hindu Temple*, London 1977

Mitra, D, *Buddhist Monuments*, Calcutta 1971

Reuther, O, *Indische Palaste und Wohnhauser*, Berlin 1925

Rowland, B, *The Art and Architecture of India*, London 1967

Soundara Rajan, K V, *Indian Temple Styles*, Delhi 1972

Srinivasan, K R, *Temples of South India*, Delhi 1972

Tadgell, Christopher, *The History of Architecture in India*, London 1990

Tillotson, G H R, *The Rajput Palaces,* New Haven and London 1987

index

maps

THE INDIAN SUB-CONTINENT

GANDHARA

PAKISTAN

RAJASTHAN

GWALIOR
BUNDELKHAND
MALWA

BENGAL

GUJARAT

MAGADHA

KATHIAWAR

ORISSA

THE DECCAN

Arabian Sea

INDIAN OCEAN

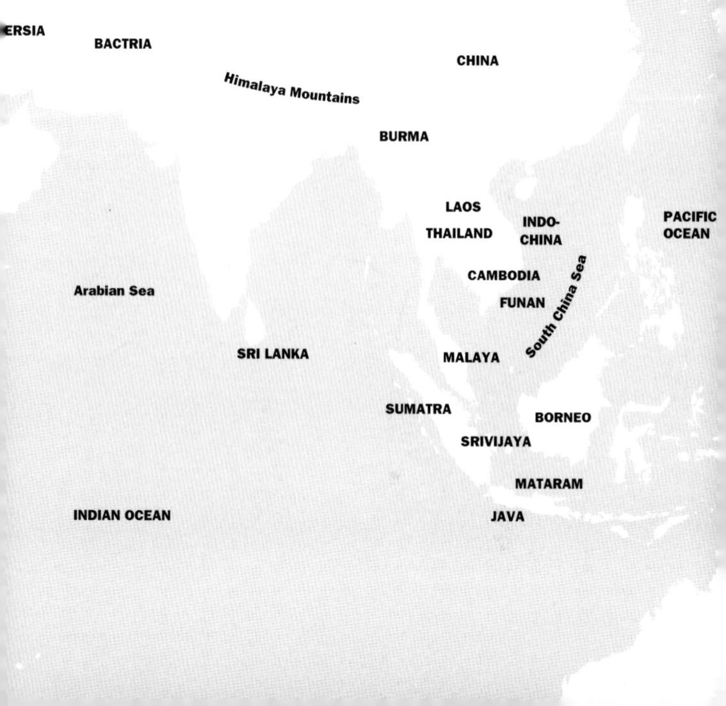

PERSIA

BACTRIA

Himalaya Mountains

CHINA

BURMA

LAOS

THAILAND

INDO-
CHINA

PACIFIC
OCEAN

CAMBODIA

Arabian Sea

FUNAN

South China Sea

SRI LANKA

MALAYA

SUMATRA

BORNEO

SRIVIJAYA

MATARAM

INDIAN OCEAN

JAVA